What Your Colleagues Are Saying ...

Anyone interested in teaching writing should read this excellent book on providing feedback—the ideas presented by Patty McGee can not only change how students write, but just as importantly help them develop an I-can-do attitude when it comes to writing.

—**STEVE GRAHAM**, EdD, Warner Professor, Mary Lou Fenton Teachers College, Arizona State University, and Editor of *Best Practices in Writing Instruction*

What happens when you combine Carol Dweck's concept of growth mindset, John Hattie's findings on visible learning, and decades of writing research and theory? This resource. Patty McGee provides a much-needed process for creating a nurturing environment that develops students' positive writing identities and skills while building on their strengths. Through this powerful feedback lens, teachers gain a wider view of how to empower novice writers to take risks, set goals, make choices, and reflect on their progress and writing.

—**TERRELL A. YOUNG**, EdD, Professor Brigham Young University

Patty McGee should be called the "writer whisperer." She expertly walks us through the sensitive and beautiful process of teaching young writers rather than just teaching writing skills. Through actual examples and real-world illustrations she demonstrates how to uncover and foster the natural writer in every child. She weaves cogent learning theory, essential character development, and cohesive instructional strategies into her process for teaching all young writers. She offers brilliant advice for helping struggling writers, accomplished writers, and all those in between. I can't help but wonder how much better I would be as a writer if I could have experienced the kinds of constructive feedback, risk taking, and nurturing Patty McGee so eloquently presents.

—**DEBBIE SILVER**, Co-Author of *Teaching Kids to Thrive*

At long last! After reading this book, I feel more able to break the habit of constantly assessing student writing and instead allow students to guide me in giving them effective feedback. Patty McGee has a warm and encouraging tone and makes a brilliant case for how we can transform students' writing by crafting a warm and admiring tone of our own to use with our writers. And she shares ways of nurturing students that are unintimidating and doable for a broad range of teaching styles, from considering each writer's identity to showing our own vulnerabilities and more. But what I love is that the book isn't all warm fuzzies—it's forceful, razor sharp about what does and doesn't develop writers' strengths, and filled with practicality and options. The charts, step-by-steps, student samples, and exemplary language make implementing the ideas immediate. No matter what your school curriculum or situation, Patty McGee helps you see how you can incorporate the type of feedback and teaching that will transform writers and their writing. The entire time I was reading this book, I kept thinking to myself how easily I could switch out the words "writing" and "writer" for "reading" and "reader" and see the same transformation in my reading instruction and in my readers.

—**JENNIFER MEYER,** Literacy Coach
Daniel Webster School, New Rochelle, NY

When reading a professional text, I have come to expect one of three things: a book with a solid pedagogy, a book with practicality, or, on a lucky day, one with passion. It's a rare gem when a text has all three qualities and Patty McGee's *Feedback That Moves Writers Forward* is one of these precious finds. From the first chapter onward Patty shows us what feedback is and what it is *not*. Feedback is individualized, specific, timely, and—ultimately—what will motivate our students to risk take, goal set, and find their unique voices as writers. Through vignettes, model work, and transcripts, Patty breaks down the process of incorporating feedback into a literacy classroom. You can take her ideas and the next day go into your classroom and try it out. This book reminds novice and seasoned teachers alike of the power of our words. What we say to our students, how we say it, is *everything*.

—**KATIE MCGRATH,** Sixth-Grade Teacher
West Brook Middle School, Paramus, NJ

Feedback That Moves Writers Forward

© Rick Harrington Photography

For Frankie, Jack, and Shannon,
my greatest treasures

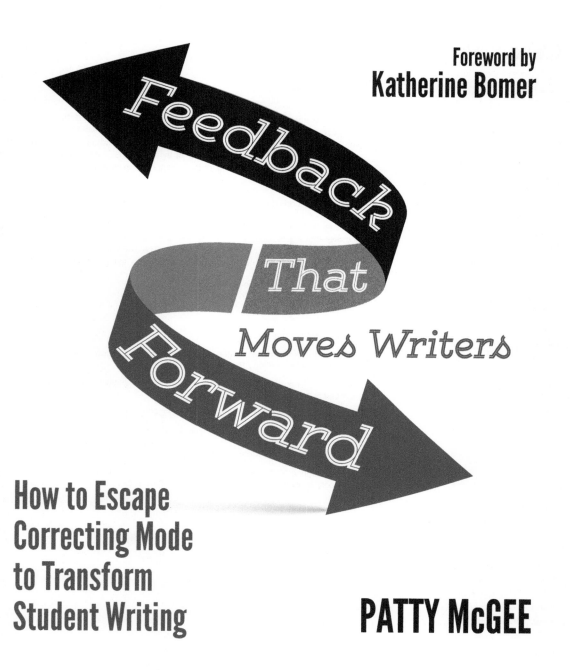

Foreword by
Katherine Bomer

Feedback That Moves Writers Forward

How to Escape Correcting Mode to Transform Student Writing

PATTY McGEE

http://resources.corwin.com/McGee-Feedback

CL CORWIN
LITERACY

FOR INFORMATION:

Corwin

A SAGE Company

2455 Teller Road

Thousand Oaks, California 91320

(800) 233-9936

www.corwin.com

SAGE Publications Ltd.

1 Oliver's Yard

55 City Road

London EC1Y 1SP

United Kingdom

SAGE Publications India Pvt. Ltd.

B 1/I 1 Mohan Cooperative Industrial Area

Mathura Road, New Delhi 110 044

India

SAGE Publications Asia-Pacific Pte. Ltd.

3 Church Street

#10-04 Samsung Hub

Singapore 049483

Senior Program Director and Publisher: Lisa Luedeke

Senior Acquisitions Editor: Wendy Murray

Editorial Development Manager: Julie Nemer

Editorial Assistant: Nicole Shade

Production Editor: Melanie Birdsall

Copy Editor: Talia Greenberg

Typesetter: C&M Digitals (P) Ltd.

Proofreader: Jeff Bryant

Indexer: Molly Hall

Cover and Interior Designer: Anupama Krishnan

Marketing Manager: Rebecca Eaton

Fundamental icons throughout the book are courtesy of clipart.com.

All trademarks depicted within this book, including trademarks appearing as part of a screenshot, figure, or other image, are included solely for the purpose of illustration and are the property of their respective holders. The use of the trademarks in no way indicates any relationship with, or endorsement by, the holders of said trademarks.

Printed in the United States of America

Library of Congress Cataloging-in-Publication Data

Names: McGee, Patricia, author.

Title: Feedback that moves writers forward: how to escape correcting mode to transform student writing / Patty McGee.

Description: Thousand Oaks, California : Corwin, 2017. | Includes bibliographical references and index.

Identifiers: LCCN 2016045811 | ISBN 9781506349923 (pbk. : alk. paper)

Subjects: LCSH: English language—Composition and exercises—Study and teaching. | English language—Rhetoric—Study and teaching. | Communication in education. | Effective teaching. | Feedback (Psychology)

Classification: LCC PE1404 .M393 2017 | DDC 808/.042071—dc23
LC record available at https://lccn.loc.gov/2016045811

This book is printed on acid-free paper.

17 18 19 20 21 10 9 8 7 6 5 4 3 2 1

DISCLAIMER: This book may direct you to access third-party content via web links, QR codes, or other scannable technologies, which are provided for your reference by the author(s). Corwin makes no guarantee that such third-party content will be available for your use and encourages you to review the terms and conditions of such third-party content. Corwin takes no responsibility and assumes no liability for your use of any third-party content, nor does Corwin approve, sponsor, endorse, verify, or certify such third-party content.

Contents

© Rick Harrington Photography

© Rick Harrington Photography

List of Companion Website Tools

Note From the Publisher: The author has provided video and web content throughout the book that is available to you through QR (quick response) codes. To read a QR code, you must have a smartphone or tablet with a camera. We recommend that you download a QR code reader app that is made specifically for your phone or tablet brand.

 Access the following resources at
http://resources.corwin.com/McGee-Feedback

Tools and Handouts

Feedback Tracker

Writer's Notebook Feedback and Grades

Grading Framework

What's Your Writing Identity?

Language That Fosters a Supportive Tone

Tips for Goal-Centered Conferring and Structuring Feedback Time

Underwater Mindframes: Ideas and Language to Share With Students

Language That Supports Risk Taking With Idea Generation

Language That Supports a Writer's Risk Taking During Revision

Language That Fosters Trust

Choices for Structure in Informational Writing

Choices for Elaborating in Narrative Writing

Choices for Elaborating in Informational Writing

Choices for Elaborating in Opinion/Argument Writing

Grammar and Choice Feedback Chart

The Iceberg Illusion

Video Clips

Feedback Fundamental: Set the Tone

Alejandro

Casey

Tia

How This Book Works for Writing Teachers of All Stripes

This book is a collection of many wonderful things created by some out-of-this-world teachers and a few of my own designs. It is more than any one teacher can do in a year, so I hereby bless you to use its chapters in any order you wish, at any pace you need. I also wrote it so that it really can work for teachers in a range of school settings and writing frameworks. At the end of the day, programs and pedagogies don't teach, teachers do. As I hope this book will prove, what matters most is the clarity of the instruction, the authenticity and sheer hours of writing, and the quality of the feedback to student writers. These attributes can occur in many classroom environments. Following are a few suggestions for ideas most ripe for transplanting.

If You Currently Use a Writing Program

Many of us work in schools that have purchased a writing program. What typifies these resources is that so much is already decided for the teacher and students, including writing topics, structures, and elaboration techniques. Overall, the program's materials drive the expectations and outcomes.

Common Challenges	Use This Book to Augment . . .
Prescriptive programs may teach writing as a process, but sometimes in implementation, the process becomes lockstep rather than recursive in nature, and students are shepherded from one phase to another with little sense of choice or agency.	Students' understanding of writing as a process of planning, drafting, revising, and editing, and the idea that *they* as writers choose strategies to use at each phase.
Prescriptive approaches by design do not encourage creative risk taking by writers, because the topics, structures, and final writing product are predetermined.	Students' risk taking with content, craft, and expression of style, even when writing in a low-choice context.
Programs may have clear goals, tasks, expectations for success, and rubrics to guide student writers' learning, but lack instruction and mindset around helping students to define goals unique to them.	Students' motivation to set personal, meaningful goals within the expectations of the program, unit, or writing task.
Students are expected to proceed at the same pace, attending to the same thing, and even if there is some differentiation guidance it is far from the differentiation and student-driven choice afforded by a workshop model.	Students' choices and adaptations within the expectations of the program, unit, or writing task.
The teacher is often expected to correct the grammar and conventions for accuracy, and these corrections are evident in the final piece.	Students' reflecting on the writing mechanics and conventions they applied as part of the same process of reflection when they name what they learned from the experience that can be used in other writing pieces and settings.

If You Currently Use an Organic Approach

An organic approach is one in which the students have most of the ownership over what happens in a writing experience. In essence, it's the writing workshop model, and sometimes called "process writing." The teachers may not have many concrete resources except themselves, their students, and some general unit plans.

Common Challenges	Use This Book to Augment . . .
With students at various stages of planning, drafting, revising, and editing writing, teachers may fall into an "air-traffic controller" mode instead of acting as mentor providing valuable feedback at each stage.	Feedback that is attuned to process of writing and that helps students apply strategies for planning, drafting, revising, and editing.
Grades, outside pressures, and curriculum demands can undermine the spirit of creative risk taking in a classroom writing environment, which in turn can undermine young writers' motivation.	Instruction and feedback that encourages students' risk taking with content, craft, and expression of style even if the lessons/units you implement focus on particular genres or skills.
Goal setting sometimes takes on a generic or perfunctory quality, and relates to trying a new genre or getting a piece done on time.	An increase in students' motivation to set personal, meaningful goals and to work to meet those goals, both writing- and writer-centered, and celebrate their personal growth through reflection.
Writing workshop/organic models operate most successfully with a high degree of student choice, but teachers may not recognize the degree to which they are still making too many of the decisions.	Student choice that arises from within the learner rather than in response to a menu of options you provide. Students choose what to work on in terms of topic, structure, grammar, conventions, elaboration details, and sometimes even genre.

Foreword

I met Patty McGee when we were both teaching sessions at the Paramus Summer Writing Institute in New Jersey. Instantly, I felt certain she was the little sister I never had. For one thing, we share the delights and frustrations of having curly hair (though hers is that impossibly bright, white-like-the-sun color that I have always wanted—mine, a duller blonde).

But there is another, more critical thing we share, and that is an unshakable belief that all children can love writing and can write well, if we give them appreciative feedback on what they are already doing beautifully as writers and help them grow from those strengths. We both owe a great deal to the legacy of Donald Graves, who in his revolutionary work in the late 1970s argued that children want to write when we are fascinated by what they have to say. "Somewhere, in your stomach perhaps, you have a belief, even a fascination, that children know these things, and you can't wait to find out what they are" (Newkirk & Kittle, 2013).

Now, in *Feedback That Moves Writers Forward*, Patty both revives and reinvents how to believe in and be fascinated by children's writing.

What any writer wants more than anything is appreciative response. We want people to read or listen to our work and to gasp, weep, belly laugh, sigh, get riled up, and want to make the world a better place. Writers want feedback, and they want it to be thoughtful and positive, not punishing or evaluative.

Our young writers want the same thing—for someone to listen carefully, to notice their Herculean efforts, and to react by naming what they have accomplished, the specific beauty and brilliance that is already there.

Yet in classrooms, across generations, response to writing has been primarily evaluative—assigning a scored *value*, the way one might rate a diamond, say, or a fancy bottle of wine, to what is probably the most vulnerable activity a child does in school. A low evaluation can crush a child-like "Maggie," the third grader whose touching story Patty tells to frame this book. Whether it is a number or a letter grade, that subjective judgment has had questionable, if not utterly destructive results for the young people who are simply offering the best thinking and feeling shaped by words they can right now. It is shocking that more kids don't stage protests.

In truth, it can be hard to know what to say to children about their writing, since what we most easily notice are the errors and what is lacking. Thankfully, we now have this compendium of strategies, this one-stop shop for ways to give authentic, purposeful feedback in this amazing book by Patty McGee. With her warm, clear, and positive voice that feels like we are learning side-by-side with our sister or wise best friend, Patty guides us through the methods and means of giving "writer-centered feedback" to our student, no matter what age group we teach.

The heart of the book builds from Carol Dweck's research into the learning benefits of a growth mindset versus a fixed mindset. Patty applies Dweck's theory to helping kids find their own writing identities and giving them feedback on their process that allows for mistakes and revisions. Her chapter about how to help our "stuck" writers, for instance, offers compassionate and practical suggestions for first learning why a student is stuck, ways to help build trust between student and teacher, and then small steps to help that student find his or her voice and move forward.

The book is beautifully organized, moving through methods for assessing students' writing, giving oral and written feedback, setting up partners and small groups for peer feedback, helping students set goals, and most important, helping students reflect on their learning and self-assess. Patty writes from research into the history of writing assessment, theories of learning, and her own experience as a teacher and a professional developer. And, oh my, teachers and literacy coaches will be delighted to find dozens upon dozens of surveys, protocols, charts, and organizational tools to use immediately in their classrooms, as well as colorful and impressive samples of teacher and student work.

I predict that Patty's Chapter 2 about grading will become the resource for faculty discussions and professional development. She takes us on a little journey through the rather bleak history of grading writing, but she allows that grades still rule in most school accountability systems, and so offers alternative models. She names areas to assess, then demonstrates how we might weigh parts of the writing process and goal setting as options for "integrading" (as Patty gleefully calls it) feedback with grading. I plan to send every teacher, school faculty, and district literacy director this chapter when the topic of grading writing comes up from now on.

Our ultimate goals as writing teachers should be to create independence, even joy in student writers. Patty helps us envision the environments that will hold and sustain these goals. She tells us how crucial it is to build trust in order to grow our young writers. Trust me now when I say that Patty's book will help us reach and even transcend our hopes for all of our students.

—**KATHERINE BOMER**
Author of *The Journey Is Everything*

Acknowledgments

Thank you to my husband, Frankie, and my children, Jack and Shannon, whose dream for me was bigger than my own. You made sacrifices small and large for this book, and every writer should have a team like you behind her. My cup runneth over with gratitude and love.

Thank you to my Mom and Dad, Peter and Kay Grawehr, who made sure my family ate during my many months of working and writing, and who nourish us in so many other ways with support and love every single day.

Thank you to Corwin Literacy, and here's my checklist of gratitude:

- Wendy Murray, my deepest gratitude to you for helping me refine my vision, capture the words just shy of my grasp, and develop my own writing identity—you are the first teacher to help me do so.

- Rosanne Kurstedt, my second editor, for the consistent, thoughtful, insightful feedback at every level of this book. Your feedback made my writing evolve.

- Judy Wallis, whose insights resonate throughout the book.

- Mike Soules, Lisa Shaw, and Lisa Luedeke for dreaming big and creating Corwin Literacy.

- Rebecca Eaton for marketing that knows no bounds and who knows teachers' needs.

- Julie Nemer, Nicole Shade, Melanie Birdsall, and the many others at Corwin who make a book happen on schedule and with everything just right.

- Anupuma Krishnan for designing a knockout cover.

- Rick Harrington for the gorgeous photos that make my writing come alive.

My heartfelt thanks to the "godmothers" of this book. First, to my colleague, friend, and mentor, Gravity Goldberg. I know that this book came about because of you. From the birth of the idea to the manuscript, your guidance was priceless. Even more important, the unwavering belief you have had in me, and my work as part of your team, is what I am most grateful for, Gravity. To this book's other "godmothers," Katherine Bomer and Kathy Collins, I admire your hearts and generous approach to the world, something I have tried to emulate and capture in this book as well. Your encouragement when this book was in the newborn stage pushed me to move forward. Your books acted as mentors to me.

A big thank you to my teammates, Danielle Larsen, Laura Sarsten, Pam Koutrakos, and Julie Budzinski-Flores, who have the uncanny ability to say just the right thing at the right time, or send me words, ideas, or insights that are just what I am searching for.

I also thank teachers Kim Niland and Denise Zalis who shared their insights and expertise with me after reviewing an early draft of this book. The perspective from thoughtful, invested teachers like you helped make this both practical and relevant.

I thank my dear friend Julie McAuley, who as a colleague and friend, celebrates every milestone with me, and has been my biggest cheerleader in writing this book. A truer, kinder, more motivating friend cannot be found. And to all of my friends who have celebrated this new world of authorship with me: Carley Anne Tsaglos, Dana Sir, Ally Murphy, Leslie Galioto, Jeannine Deramo, Michele Perez, Laura Wood, and friends from my hometown, I am filled with gratitude.

I thank the Northern Valley for the opportunity to cut my teeth in the world of literacy coaching. Linda Mayer, my friend, teacher, and lifelong mentor—from my years as a high school student with you, to my early years in teaching, to the early work in professional learning, and now as an author—you have not only revealed to me my own possibilities, you have given me the foundation and road map to take the journey. You have shaped me and my life, and I thank you. To my former team at the Northern Valley Curriculum Center, Bob Price, Kathleen O'Flynn, Jon Regan, Debbie Stevens, Diane Blaskewicz, Jeannine Deramo, and Laura Wood, I appreciate the years we worked together. I also thank the schools of the

Northern Valley, especially Harrington Park, where, thanks to Adam Fried, my literacy learning sprouted and grew, and where we were able to capture the photos for this book in Jennifer Allen, Marianne Grocela, Kim Niland, and Allison Gee's classrooms. My teamwork with Jess Nitzberg, the principal there, has been a shining gem of learning. Our collaboration has been my favorite so far, my friend, and I draw on it daily. I am grateful to Betty Johnson, my first-grade teacher and later my principal in my first teaching job, and all of my other Norwood colleagues, who have shaped my teaching. I am also grateful to the many teachers I worked with in the "Valley" and the learning I have gained from them all, there are too many to name.

Many thanks to the Milken Family Foundation, which on the earlier side of my teaching life, shocked me with the award of awards for teachers and solidified in me the belief that if I follow my passions as a teacher, I have the ability, talent, and backing to take the next steps.

I also thank the teachers I have studied and are collaborators in this book. Their work with children day in and day out is the work of heroes! This book would be without heart if not for their contributions. Thank you, Laura Sarsten, Pam Koutrakos, Courtney Rejent, Lena Gurioan, Nancy Costanzo, Lesa Jezequel, Brianne Annitti, and Rob Karklin.

I also must thank the kids in my life. As one student whispered to me as I entered a classroom to study, "I think you'll be inspired here. I've seen what they can do." Incredibly true words—I found inspiration, and I imagine all the readers will too.

Why Feedback Matters as Much as (or More Than!) the Lessons We Teach

Part 1

Chapter 1

Effective Feedback in Writing

What We Know Works

I invite you into this book by telling you three stories about three very different writers. I wonder if, after reading these, you might have a story of your own?

First, there's Maggie, a third grader I met recently when I was invited to model conferring in front of a dozen teachers. I am guessing you have a Maggie in your classroom, or maybe a few Maggies. She's the writer who struggles and shuts down, the writer who keeps you and her other teachers up at night. She is one of those writers who folds into themselves when it is time to write, her body hunching down and her facial expression becoming an armor; it is as though almost every word she etches on the page causes pain. She is also the kind of student who the teachers usually ask me to work with when I am in their classrooms.

When I pulled up my chair to talk to Maggie, I worried that she might cry; she was clearly uncomfortable with so many eyes on her. She sat with her head tilted down, her writing pencil frozen over her notebook. She was trying out the strategy from a lesson I had just taught. I waited, resisting the urge to speak. She seemed stuck. I waited.

Maggie turned the page toward the beginning of her notebook, where she had a few sketches paired with some writing.

This is a strength, Maggie! I thought, looking at her downturned face. "Maggie, I see you are a writer who sketches to really picture what is happening before you write. There are so many authors who use their notebooks this way. I'd love to be able to share one of the strategies I learned from them with you."

Maggie lifted her head and looked me in the eye. Her shoulders seemed to relax, and she nodded. I could tell she was ready to try something new. I shared a sketching strategy with her, one where she might sketch each part of the story she was writing as a way to help plan her writing. To my joy and relief, she jumped right into it, a broad smile spreading across her face. At that moment, I looked up at the teachers. They all had tears in their eyes. Later I learned that Maggie almost never smiles.

This experience is not new to me—I work with students like Maggie all of the time with a similar emotional response from the teachers, followed by the question, "What did you do to make that happen? I want to try that with another student." I help teachers to realize that the breakthrough occurs every time not because of any writing strategy, but because of my tone, and because I build on a student's strength as the way forward. This is what causes the shift; this is what creates an openness to learning and trying something new. In my 9 years as a literacy consultant, and 13 years prior that as a classroom teacher, I have come to realize teachers want—and students need—a new type of conversation about writing. Before we delve more deeply into this proposition, I'll share the second story. This one is my own.

In a writing workshop by the inspiring Ralph Fletcher a few years back, Ralph asked the audience of hundreds of teachers to raise their hands if they considered themselves readers. Most hands went up, including my own. He then asked, "How many of you consider your-selves writers, or even like to write?" A dozen or so hands rose, but not mine. I looked around, oddly comforted by the fact that I was not the only teacher who seemed to be doing their best to fake the love of writing for students. Yet, most of all, I was shocked. There we were, in a workshop on teaching writing, a subject most of us taught every single day, and only a few of us identified ourselves as writers. Had we not all spent at least 17 years in school learning to write (even more with the many advanced degrees in the room)? Where along the way did we lose the belief that we are writers? Or is it that we never had that belief in the first place?

I'm guessing that for many of us, the loss of faith in our ability to write is gradual, like beach erosion. Often in school, year after year, we get hit by a steady surf of corrections, comments, and grades. But I imagine, too, that many of us can point to a time when we felt literally knocked down as a writer. For me, it was when I participated in a summer institute and submitted a piece of writing to read aloud at a final writing celebration.

It was a piece about my father, when he was still unconscious after triple-bypass surgery, and I sat at his bedside, late into the night, reflecting on memories. To my surprise and delight, it was selected. I was asked to meet with someone on staff who would help me trim my piece down. We sat in chairs right next to the stage. She flicked a red marker pen like a baton as she skimmed my piece, and then she quickly put a line through one of the paragraphs, said, "Take this part out. It is trite," and handed the piece back to me.

Trite. It was as though the experience itself was under attack, as though my feelings about my father were a dime-a-dozen, cliché. I looked at my paper. A thick red line now slashed through the mem-ory. I began to cry, right there next to the stage as the teachers were pouring into the auditorium. Another teacher came up to me, some-one else who had been chosen to read aloud at the celebration. She put her arm around me. "I get it," she whispered. "They did the same to my piece. The same thing to me."

Now, the third story: My 77-year-old dad was pleased as punch that his daughter was writing a book—this book—yet he couldn't really explain what I was writing about to his buddies. He arrived at my house with a pen and pad in hand to jot down exactly what my (this) book was all about. Before I explained, I asked him to describe his experience in school when his teachers gave him feedback on his writing. He said, "They used a red pen to correct, and there was more red pen than my pen!" (He thought that was his best joke of the day.) I smiled and then asked him, "So what do you think about yourself as a writer now, and what did you think then?" He laughed even harder and said, "It made me realize I am a pretty crappy writer!"

On the contrary, my dad is not a "crappy" writer. I have little treasures of notes and letters he has written to me over the years, and he is a guest preacher at a church in the area. He *can* write; he just doesn't believe he can. And I wonder what would have gone differently for him had he believed himself a writer.

Okay, three stories, representing three generations: Maggie, myself, and my father. Add to these three your own, and the tales of so many others, and we can clearly see the damaging results that error-focused, "fix-it" feedback can potentially have across a life-time. I wrote this book to try to offer a practical, transformative approach to feedback, so that maybe when today's students are in their 70s, fewer of them will have lived with the belief all of their lives that they cannot write.

When our students hear error-focused feedback often enough—and see it in the margins of their papers or in the comments on their digital documents—they come to believe that getting better at writing is a matter of only correcting mistakes. And worse, they often see themselves as less and less of a writer with every correction they get. Our pens may be blue or green or purple ink because some-where along the line we felt red pen comments smack of old-school correcting—but guess what? Our feedback may still be hindering, not fostering, learning. The research points to this hazard. In *Best Practices in Writing Instruction* (second edition; Graham, McArthur, and Fitzgerald) the authors state:

> Writing is hard work and learning to write well is even harder. Students are less likely to put forth their best efforts when writing or learning to write if they view the classroom

as an unfriendly, chaotic, high-risk, or punitive place. Many students evidence mental withdrawal or evasion of productive work in such situations (Hansen, 1989). This makes it especially important to develop a classroom writing environment that is interesting, pleasant, and nonthreatening, where the teacher supports students and students support each other. (pp. 12–13)

In my own action research over the years, as I examined my own practice and the work of other teachers as well as that of professional writers, I have come to believe that yes, developing nurturing writing environments is critical, but that we must start with the writer, each writer, and build the collective "we" from there. We have to first discover and develop a student's writing identity, so they can (re)define who they are and what makes them tick. And we do this through feedback that is writer-focused *and* fosters growth in writing.

Feedback: The Research Support

Feedback that is clear, timely, and relevant to the writer is central to writing development. It can shape a writer's identity and a writer's growth. "Feedback is information with which a learner can confirm, add to, overwrite, tune, or restructure information in memory, whether that information is . . . beliefs about self, or cognitive tactics and strategies" (Hattie & Timperley, 2007, p. 82). Feedback can foster in a learner a growth mindset (Dweck, 2006; 2012). An individual with a growth mindset believes that his or her skills can be grown, acquired. By contrast, those who have a fixed mindset believe ability is innate and unchangeable. Hayes (1996) describes the research of Palmquist and Young, who noted in college students the relationship between the belief that writing is an innate gift, on the one hand, and the presence of writing anxiety, on the other. They found that students who believed strongly that writing is a gift had significantly higher levels of writing anxiety and significantly lower self-assessments of their ability as writers than did other students. Think back to Maggie, and how it's almost as though I flicked a switch from fixed mindset to growth mindset by

naming her strength, and assuring her that there were strategies for her to acquire that would make her a more skilled writer.

In addition to research by Dweck and other cognitive psychologists, there is a strong research base within literacy that supports feedback as a means to help change the beliefs of individuals to motivate learning. Writing researchers at the forefront of the process theory of composition, including Janet Emig, Donald Murray, and Donald Graves, and George Hillocks and his expressive method among many others, all recognized that formal, traditional approaches to teaching writing didn't improve the quality of students' writing. Grammar, style, structure, all needed to be taught in the midst of real writing. Furthermore, to nurture risk taking, perseverance, engagement, and ownership, and in turn create passionate, invested, proficient writers, teachers needed to maximize writing as a social act. The writing workshop model bubbled up from this premise, and providing meaningful feedback while conferring with a student arose as a key practice. Donald Graves would sit beside a young writer after reading her draft and begin giving feedback by saying something like, "Wow, tell me about this!" (1983). His feedback would be based on what the young writer said. Carl Andersen opens up the mind and heart of a writer with, "How's it going?" Ralph Fletcher encourages writers to be exploring and playful to uncover their craft. And Katherine Bomer reminds us always to use feedback to preserve the writer, for writing is an act of vulnerability.

John Hattie's synthesis of more than 900 meta-analyses (2009; 2012) shows that feedback has one of the highest effects on student learning. Peter Johnston reminds us in *Opening Minds* (2012) that "The purpose of feedback is to improve conceptual understanding or increase strategic options while developing stamina, resilience, and motivation—expanding the vision of what is possible and how to get there."

Why Don't We Live the Research?

Many of us have read the groundbreaking work of Carl Andersen, Katherine Bomer, Angela Duckworth, Carol Dweck, and Ralph Fletcher—or, at the very least, share their values of growth mindset, asset-based feedback, and student-centered instruction. Yet, when it comes to what actually happens in the classroom, well-meaning teachers seem to slide into a correcting mode. Why? Somewhat ironically, I think teachers rush in to fix things because they feel so pressed for time, and under such pressure to prove their student writers' progress. Alas, it's a temporary fix.

When I was a teacher, I too would spend hours correcting student writing each night, only to find that my students never included any of those suggestions in the future. Similarly, when I met with writers and quickly fixed a piece's most obvious weaknesses, the students would bring me a next draft with those blemishes covered—but no other revisions. It was as though the piece, and the writer, never came into full bloom as the result of my feedback. Even worse, my students were often unmotivated to write, and thought of writing as a task. I was baffled.

There are many factors at work that can cause this:

- Teachers often teach the way they have been taught themselves and give feedback in the manner they have received it (McMillan, 1985). There have been few models, in our lives and in our classrooms, of giving noncorrective feedback for us to emulate.

- Teachers feel the pressure of national scrutiny and accountability. They have limited time, and the state test is looming. The testing culture often pushes teachers to abandon their values (Kohn, 2000). The standards are rigorous for argument, informational, and narrative writing, and because writing cuts across the content areas, it's the bulls-eye of the target.

- Teachers often hold a deep insecurity about their own ability to write and because of that, many teachers often have done little writing of their own in years. As a result, they are trying to guide a process they themselves don't fully understand, and

it becomes all too easy to rely on a menu of strategies rather than discover what really nourishes their student writers.

The Way Forward

Whatever the real obstacles in our path as we try to give feedback to our writers, I think the way to push these giant boulders aside is to recognize that both written and oral feedback comes down to the same thing: words, and the tone of them, that first begin with the writer within. I know: Deceptively simple solution, right? We know that our words hold great power in shaping students' beliefs about themselves as writers (Johnston, 2012). The art of teaching blends choosing the words that create literate agency with strategies that empower young writers. The key is in changing how we have the conversation, and changing the nature of the conversation.

The conversation with a student becomes an eclectic blend of razor-sharp intentionality (*Today I'm going to listen for how this student is feeling about her attention to flashback, or, today I'm watching for confidence and motivation*) and intuitive improvisation, where we gather information about a writer "in all ways"—her risk taking, her goal setting, her choices, her ability to reflect. When we attend to these four things, we are starting with the students and their identities as writers. Effective feedback synthesizes both the mindsets and the mechanics of writing. This type of feedback will make a world of difference to all our young writers, and most especially to our Maggies. In a nutshell, writING specific feedback will not flourish without involving the writERS themselves in the process. Now, let's dig into how to make this happen.

Growth Mindset and Feedback

The most significant influence on rethinking my approach to feedback was psychologist Carol Dweck's work in mindset. As I mentioned earlier, Dweck described two different types of mindsets: a fixed mindset and a growth mindset. These mindsets can impact how much one learns, how one may approach a learning experience, and whether or not a learner grows to his or her full potential. In her EdWeek blog, Dweck shared, "We found that students' mindsets—how they perceive their abilities—played a key role in their motivation and achievement, and we found that if we changed students' mindsets, we could boost their achievement" (2015). Dweck defines growth mindset as "students who believe their intelligence could be developed." With a growth mindset, a learner believes that mistakes, difficulty, and frustration are moments of learning, and persevering through those challenges makes one smarter.

Students who hold a fixed mindset believe that they are as smart as they will ever be, there is no experience that will make them smarter or stronger, and moments of frustration or difficulty only confirm this belief. I am sure you have seen such writers in your classroom. Those who say, "I am a terrible writer" and whose actions fulfill that belief. They may shut down during difficulty, rarely try something new in their writing, or avoid writing altogether. On the flip side, you may have strong writers with a fixed mindset that undermines their development as well. For example, a student might define himself as a strong writer, perhaps because teachers and parents have defined him as gifted, but in the face of difficulty or even the smallest suggestion, he may close or even break down. Or her perceived identity has been shattered; the correction or critique makes her question who she thought she was. Writers with a fixed mindset believe that their intelligence is static, and when faced with challenges, obstacles, a need for effort, criticism, or the success of others, they plateau and do not grow to their full potential. The good news is that the type of feedback we give to writers can nurture a growth over fixed mindset. When we

- celebrate mistakes as learning opportunities,
- focus on the process of learning,
- acknowledge effort that leads to learning,
- give choices of next steps when writers encounter difficulty, and
- reflect on the work of learning

our feedback supports a growth mindset (Dweck, 2015). The organization of this book will mirror this very structure.

Writers with a growth mindset believe that their intelligence can be developed, and by embracing challenges, persevering through obstacles, employing effort, learning from criticism, and finding inspiration in others, they reach higher levels of achievement.

Pam Koutrakos's Growth Mindset classroom chart

Developing Writers: Mindset, Identity, and Feedback

As you will discover in the chapters ahead, it's quite natural to focus our instruction on writer's identity, mindset, and feedback. With this focus (as opposed to trying to cover a gazillion rules or discrete skills) we can more easily layer in other components of an effective writing program: strong strategy instruction, cultivating a community of writers, sheer time spent writing, a variety of genres, wide reading of texts, word study (including vocabulary and spelling), and grammar study. This identity–mindset–feedback concept grounds instruction, affording solidly writer-centered teaching. Throughout this book, we will explore ways of fortifying this trio, so let's begin by exploring how the identity–mindset–feedback strands intertwine.

Okay, first, we *need* our writers to have a positive writing identity to truly reach their greatest potential as writers.

Examples of Positive Writing Identities	Why This Is a Positive Writing Identity
I am the type of writer who writes fiction stories but often goes on and on. I look to my teacher and peers for feedback on what really belongs. I never feel like my writing is quite complete, even at a deadline.	This writer is aware of strengths and challenges without a negativity attached. She looks for feedback from others and sees writing as an ongoing process.
I write for myself all the time at home, mostly comics. I find myself using pictures in my mind or sketches on paper when I write so I can envision my writing before I jot a single word. I often rehearse my plan or my sentences in my head before writing them down. I often get stuck and turn to other resources to get moving.	This writer is a writer in more than one setting and knows his process. He expects difficulty in writing, because writing is hard, and has a plan on how to work through the difficulty.
I jump right into writing, so I never seem to have writer's block. I am most interested in writing about marine wildlife and like to research to stay up to date. I don't like story writing as much as my opinion on why we should care for the environment.	This writer has a passion and follows it. He knows what writers do with those passions and the type of writing that fits best. He knows his habits, as well, and a larger purpose for writing.

Ellen Langer's research on mindfulness underscores the power of one's perception of one's identity. Back in 1981, Ellen and her team gathered a group of elderly men and asked them to live, for 5 days, as if it were 1959. They went so far as to create a setting that mimicked 1959, including the smallest details of music, television programs, and food. They not only surrounded these men with the world of 20 years earlier, they expected them to *live* like it was 20 years ago. The outcomes after only 5 days were pretty astounding. There was a significant increase in both their physical and cognitive abilities—essentially they became younger. It was as if the men believed themselves into a younger version of themselves, and that is what they became—healthier and smarter. An identity is pliable and influenced by the setting surrounding the writer. Our students' writing identities can have an incredible impact on their writing and "begin to grow . . . from the first mark they place on a page" (Bomer, 2010, p. 19). Students who believe themselves into stronger, proficient, and passionate writers become just that, and are happier, and therefore learning and achieving more. If we surround our students with feedback that helps them create a positive writing identity, our students learn and grow along with their writing. Feedback that supports a growth mindset and positive writer identity is the trio toward which we are striving.

Taking a Candid Look at Our Classroom Feedback

I began this journey of studying feedback long ago as a fourth-grade teacher and continue it today. My own first step was to take an honest, open look at my own feedback practices and consider their impact on my writers in both their writing and their identities as writers. I considered the type of feedback that worked for me, then I turned to student writers for their ideas, and finally I consulted the research. This chapter mirrors that same process to guide you as you consider feedback in your classroom.

Step 1: Ask Yourself Some Questions

A logical place to start is to consider what is and isn't useful, meaningful feedback in your own life. You might start to do this by reflecting on your own experiences, as a writer or otherwise, when feedback was effective and ineffective by asking yourself some reflective questions:

Questions to Ask Yourself in Considering Effective Feedback

- When did you find feedback from another person helped you grow? What qualities were included in this feedback?
- When did feedback feel focused to help you accomplish your goals and purpose? When did it not?
- When feedback was effective, what happened to you? To what you were working on?
- How can these answers help us rethink feedback with our students?

Underlying Beliefs

- Feedback has been a powerful shaper of who you are and what you believe, or don't believe, about yourself in the many facets of your life.
- Teachers have the power to shape students' beliefs about themselves through the feedback we choose (Johnston, 2004).

The choice is yours.

Step 2: Ask Your Kids Questions and Study Their Answers

Another way to think about feedback and its impact on the writer's identity is to ask students similar questions in order to gauge what feedback is most useful as well as to begin to uncover the writer's identity or mindset. This might sound like asking the reflective questions above or may follow a "request for feedback on feedback" survey. I tried the latter. I polled students for their advice on feedback and then looked closely at their reactions to begin to uncover their identity and mindset. I have included some of the student responses that I received and you may as well, and my analysis of what this means in terms of the writer's identity, mindset, and feedback. A disclaimer: Some of the student responses sound fabricated, I realize. Some of the more than 60 responses were from some very sophisticated writers and thinkers, and so their responses may sound well beyond what one may expect from a third- through eighth grader. I assure you, I have simply copied and pasted a sample response into the following chart for our study.

Feedback Type	Description	What Writers Have Said	My Hunches About This Writer
Picking up a (red) pen and correcting the writing for the student.	The teacher reads over the student's writing, making corrections for her, changing sentences around, leaving notes in the margin.	I don't like this because I would rather the teacher give me advice than to just go ahead and change my writing.	This writer owns her writing and is open to feedback.
Only giving feedback at the end of the process when a grade is involved.	A paper is turned in and the teacher takes a while reading, correcting, and writing notes to the student.	Not helpful, because if the teacher is correcting the student at the end, the student is not getting anything out of it, just a bad grade. Maybe the student would learn more if the teacher went over the paper with the student who wrote it.	This writer is looking for support through the process, which shows a disposition toward a growth mindset and the work it takes to learn.
Peer-to-peer editing. Asking students to edit each other's work.	Students sit down for a length of time with each other, pass each other their writing, and proceed to correct any editing errors.	I don't like it, because even though we feel we are right, we aren't really always the best advice givers.	This writer is realistic about the limitations of peer-to-peer feedback, but also indicates a tendency toward a fixed mindset.
Expecting all writing to be done outside the classroom and turning in a completed piece.	An assignment is given with a due date, never to be seen before that time.	If a student only is able to write an assignment out of school, the teacher will never be able to teach the writers what to improve on and their writing will stay as good as it started, not better.	This writer is open to feedback and looking to improve his writing.

Feedback Type	Description	What Writers Have Said	My Hunches About This Writer
Giving feedback only on the writing, not about the writer.	The teacher gives feedback about voice, elaboration, and structure, but not about the habits or practices a writer needs.	The teacher should not only give feedback about the writing but also about the student too because it will help improve their confidence.	This writer, whether realizing it or not, feels the writer–writing connection.
Focusing on what is "wrong."	The teacher gives feedback only on what is not right about the piece.	This is unhelpful because if you just always hear negative things about your writing piece you will feel discouraged and won't reach your true limits. You will do less than you can because you don't think you could do better if you tried.	Again, a writer who sees the importance of confidence and strength in the creation of writing. The writer is essential.
Giving feedback on everything possible in one sitting—structure, focus, grammar, conventions, elaboration, etc.	The teacher sits with a student and shows him everything he can possibly do to improve the writing.	Not helpful, we would comprehend the nomenclature better if it was segregated into increments. (Disclaimer: I realize this does not sound like a child, but I had to include it because it was Darren, a sixth grader, and he knocked my socks off with his word choice!)	This writer is a risk taker with word choice! Seems like an intuitive old soul.

I also polled students with what I would consider nontraditional feedback practices (those whose popularity began only a generation or two ago). Here is what they had to say:

Feedback Type	Description	What Writers Have Said	My Hunches About This Writer
Meeting with students one on one about their writing.	The teacher sits one on one with a student, asks the students questions about their writing, their practices, and their goals. Together they decide what to work on and the teacher explicitly teaches and coaches the student as the student tries it.	Helpful, because the teacher shows that they care for the student and the goals that the student is trying to accomplish.	This writer is open to feedback and open to growth. This student sounds like an instinctual goal setter in writing.
Feedback throughout the process.	The teacher meets with the student periodically throughout the writing process to give specific feedback.	If there is a recurring issue with their writing that would otherwise make the piece splendid, then the teacher should make sure that it is not only noticed but also fixed.	Clearly, this student has a command of beautiful writing and word selection (as seen just in this response), but I sense a bit of a fixed mindset creeping in as well as a writing, not writer, centered expectation of feedback.
The teacher taking on the role of a fellow or mentor writer in the classroom.	The teacher shares their thinking process, their writing process, and shows how they work through struggles.	It imitates how a student may encounter a problem, like what to write for the next sentence, and shows how to move through these issues to improve the writing overall.	This writer finds a model of process useful for his learning and his writing development.

Feedback Type	Description	What Writers Have Said	My Hunches About This Writer
Giving feedback on both the writing and writer.	The teacher gives feedback about voice, elaboration, structure, as well as about the habits or practices a writer needs.	Helpful, since both sides really need to be considered when writing something. The writing is obviously very important to fix and learn more about, but the writer serves just as big an importance in that state.	This writer is not fearful of opening up to feedback about herself and sees the clear connection between the writer and the writing.
Focusing on what is working and the next steps.	The teacher gives feedback on the strengths of the writing as well as what the writer is ready to try next.	You can see what you are good at, but also what you can improve on aside from your strengths. Helping with what the writer is ready to try next helps to see where they are trying to go with their work.	This writer instinctively knows that writers learn from strengths and also holds a growth mindset approach to continuous learning.

Here is the survey I used if you would like to use it as well, or use it as a template for your own survey: http://goo.gl/forms/OKhCuishzC

As I look across the feedback from the students, I have learned that there are definite feedback preferences, mindsets, and identities for the majority of young writers.

Step 3: Pull It All Together: What We Know, What Students Say, and Research

The last layer to consider about feedback is the research that addresses the qualities of feedback that support a growth mindset and a positive writing identity.

- **Provide specific feedback:** Praise such as "well done" is too general to be of use. What was done well? What are next steps? When we name what students are doing, almost doing, and not yet doing, along with suggestions for next steps, our young writers know exactly what we mean and where they can proceed (Hattie & Timperley, 2007). This specificity supports a growth mindset, nurtures a writer's identity, and adds a focus to feedback.

- **Offer timely feedback:** Feedback given immediately, or as soon as possible, significantly improves performance (Opitz, Ferdinand, & Mecklinger, 2011). This is true in any learning experience, including writing. While it is impossible to provide immediate feedback to all of our students all of the time, we know that waiting until writing is completed and published is too late. We need to give feedback throughout the process in specific, writer-centered, digestible ways.

- **Be clear and offer "just right" feedback:** We must strike the right tone with our feedback. Our young writers, according to Edward Deci (Ryan and Deci, 2000), do not flourish if they are too closely monitored, believe that feedback is meant to control them, or feel as though this is part of some competition. We strive to find the "sweet spot" of feedback: not too harsh, not too general, and not too ambitious.

- **Support the writer:** Don Graves so often reminded teachers that we teach writers—not writing. When choosing feedback in writing it must be to support the writer in owning their own learning and making choices on next steps—again supporting the positive growth of the writer's identity. Our writers need to know where they are in the learning process and where they still need to go.

- **Match feedback to writers' goals:** Tailoring feedback to student goals, as we will explore in Chapters 5 and 6, has a strong impact on student learning. In fact, according to John Hattie (2009; 2012) in *Visible Learning*, among all of the choices we can make as teachers, goals and feedback can have some of the greatest impact on student learning. (They made his top 10 list!) Much, much more on goals in Chapter 5.

Making Space and a Place for Effective Feedback

If your classroom is like most, you are crunched for time with a large class and are likely wondering where you can squeeze in as much effective feedback that supports a growth mindset and a writer's positive identity. How is it possible to give the sort of feedback that is specific, timely, writer-centered, customized, and goal-centered? Since you cannot make more time appear or shrink your class size, you must work with what you do have control over: how to spend the time you do have.

The first step in deciding how to spend the time you do have is to first identify what *you* value in writing instruction and design your time so it reflects your values. Feedback won't thrive unless we are clear on our overall beliefs, and have daily schedules, routines, and writing experiences that reflect these stances. As I said at the outset, teachers can be brilliant writing teachers when they use a scripted writing program, and they can be brilliant in a workshop setting. But they are brilliant because they are *clear* about what writing is, what writers need to develop, and consistent in how they guide students toward expectations. So in this crash course, I'm going to focus on two things: what writing is and how the classroom environment supports it.

What Does It Take to Write, Anyway?

There is no simple answer to this question, though there are consistent instructional practices that research has shown work. These are practices that I have personally used in my own classroom. Even more, these are practices I have witnessed in the most successful writing classrooms—those places where students gain incredible confidence and skill in writing despite the class size or demographic, the writing program or approach.

First, consider what writing is and what is needed from writers, as described in the seminal text, *Best Practices in Writing Instruction* (Graham, MacArthur, & Fitzgerald, 2013):

> Writing is "a goal-directed and self-sustained cognitive activity requiring the skillful management of the writing environment;

the constraints imposed by the writing topic; the intentions of the writer(s); and the process, knowledge and skills in composing. Writers must juggle and master a commanding array of skills, knowledge, and processes, including knowledge about topic and genre; strategies for planning, drafting, revising, editing, and publishing text; as well as the skills needed to craft and transcribe ideas into sentences that convey the author's intended meaning. (p. 8)

Such complex work for any writer, especially the young writers in our classrooms! In essence, assert Graham and Harris (2013), there are basically two viewpoints—those theories and researchers who focus on how context shapes writing, and those who focus on the motivational aspects. My practice, and this book, blends both camps.

The Best Practice Classroom: Environments and Routines

Below are five research-supported essentials, then, in creating classrooms that not only support the complicated work of writing, but also build in space for feedback.

- **Authentic audience-based writing experiences:** When students write with an immediate, compelling purpose (and go beyond thinking of writing as a task to complete), and see writing as a chance to share their voice with an intended audience, writers are invested and motivated.

- **Goals that stretch each writer with support to reach those goals:** Writers set their sights on something that improves both their writing and their writing skills, with feedback that is centered around reaching these goals.

- **Self-regulation in writing experiences with timely feedback:** Writers own their process, make choices about their writing, and are given—and give themselves—feedback on those choices.

- **Routines and structures that promote writing and interactions with other writers:** Writing classrooms create daily routines, including how a writing session runs, the way writers give feedback to each other, how a teacher–student conversation or conference goes, and how to make independent choices (i.e., what to do when "done").

- **An environment that supports risk taking and reflection:** The writer must have an opportunity to try something new, with a sense of safety in a low-stakes setting, and reflect on these risks to deepen learning and transfer this learning to future, often high-stakes situations.

What Can Stay/What Can Go

We cannot be sure that our students' writing identities are being tended to unless we make the space for effective feedback. Here is a list of suggestions on how to make time by limiting or eliminating the feedback that is not effective and creating spaces for meaningful feedback.

Consider Limiting or Eliminating ...	Consider Adding ...
• Long, whole group lessons unless they are launching a unit of study. This is any more than a quarter of your writing time.	• Goal setting
• Lengthy conversations with one student about multiple corrections	• Peer-to-peer feedback
• The red pen (or whatever color it might be)	• Daily, preserved time for teacher/student, one-on-one feedback
• The virtual red pen (correcting verbally)	• Independent choice making by students
• Waiting until the end of the writing process to give feedback	• Authentic writing projects
• Worksheets or other task-completion activities used in lieu of writing projects review/checking, daily quizzes, daily oral language	• Writing clubs and small-group instruction
• Daily test prep	• A toolkit for yourself to give feedback on the spot

Let's imagine the chart above in action. Following are two scenarios of a writing class. Both classes are 60 minutes long and include 20 students. Notice the differences in the choices and the spaces they create for feedback.

Classroom A

The first 15 minutes: The writing period begins. Students look up at the board for the Daily Oral Language (DOL) activity of the day. They write down the sentences as they are displayed with incorrect grammar and conventions and then make corrections. Once everyone has completed the DOL for the day, one student at a time goes to the Smart Board to show one correction and explain why he made it. This continues until all corrections are made accurately.

The next 15 minutes: Students take out their grammar homework and review the answers. Students make corrections while the teacher gives the answers. They are assigned and explained the homework for that night.

The next 10 minutes: A quiz is passed out on subject and predicate. The students are to underline the subject and circle the predicate for 10 sentences. If they finish early, they read quietly to themselves.

The final 20 minutes: Students hear a lesson on personal narrative writing and adding detail during the revision process. They watch the teacher add detail to a sample piece, they add details to another sample piece together as a class, and then they go back into their own writing for the last 5 minutes of the lesson to see where they can add detail. The teacher circulates the room and adds a check mark to the top of the writing if a detail has been used. The students move onto another subject.

Classroom B

The first 10 minutes: Students engage in a lesson on personal narrative writing that focuses on adding detail during the revision process. The teacher models briefly and the students try it in their own writing.

The next 25 minutes: Students work on their own independent writing projects in personal narrative and have opportunities to *apply* their learning. They start by sharing with their partners or writing clubs their plan for that day. They look back at their personal goals and the goals for the unit as a reminder. They write. The teacher circulates with a stool and a conferring toolkit. The teacher revisits the student's goals and then offers **feedback** on those goals, about 5 minutes a student, meeting with a quarter of the class.

The next 10 minutes: Writing clubs or partnerships come together to share the work they have done so far as well as their goals to give **feedback** to one another. They make a plan on what writing they will do for homework. The teacher circulates and gives **feedback** on the homework choices.

The last 15 minutes: Students study the use of subjects and predicates in a mentor text in clubs or partnerships. They create a list of rules that the author has followed in their use of subjects and predicates. The teacher circulates to give **feedback** on their inquiry. The students move onto another subject.

As we compare the two classrooms through the lens of feedback, it is obvious that the teacher in Classroom A allows no time to give feedback to writers aside from 5 minutes toward the very end. Classroom B is designed so that feedback happens daily. These examples illustrate the need to make choices in building a space and place for feedback. Teaching is personal and our choices are made with the best intentions, so letting go of some beloved practices can be hard. Take a look at your own classroom and consider changes you would like to make. I have a few pointers:

1. During a class, take a moment to jot about how much time you spent on different writing experiences. Do this a few times to notice patterns and possible spaces to build in opportunities for feedback.

2. Watch your students closely. Are they learning or completing? In other words, have they engaged in an experience where they will learn something new, or are they working to complete a worksheet, assignment, or task? Is there intent to complete or to learn from the task? If they are completing over learning, you may consider supporting a different way writers approach their work.

3. Watch students closely again. This time notice how much time they spend listening or watching a grownup and how much time they spend engaged in their own writing.

4. Do not feel you need to do a complete overhaul. Some teachers find it easier to go full tilt and come into a new school year or semester, but you can take it bit by bit. Perhaps you might set a goal for yourself like carving out 10 minutes to meet with students daily or build in 5 minutes a day for student-to-student feedback. Then let it grow as you are ready.

5. Reflect on the outcomes of the changes you make. Notice what is happening to your students and yourself. Celebrate the steps you and your students have made.

6. Ask a trusted colleague to visit and give you feedback and suggestions.

7. Make what you value visible every day. If you value conversations with students, put that on your desk, by the clock, on your notebook, or wherever you will be reminded to make choices that support your greatest value.

Wrapping It Up

Once we make space for the sort of feedback that helps writers develop a positive writing identity and growth mindset, beautiful things begin to happen. We teachers find many more moments of joy as we watch our young writers strengthen their writing and their writing identity (who wouldn't love more moments of joy in the classroom?!). With the writer's identity at the heart of our instruction, this book will illustrate ways the writer and writing are connected and grow together through feedback that supports risk taking, goal setting, choice making, and reflecting in practical, impactful ways.

But before we study all the ways we can offer feedback, let's reconcile the thing that drives much of the feedback in our classrooms: grading. In the next chapter we will explore different sorts of feedback that nurture a writer's identity, especially in a grade-driven culture.

Chapter 2

"Integrading"
How to Live in a Grading World and Still Give Feedback

When it comes to the discipline of writing, grades create utter chaos for students and teachers.

—Katherine Bomer, *Hidden Gems*, p. 150

Grading is a particularly prickly issue, and therefore one to work through early on in this book. Katherine Bomer is right—grades create entropy for writers—but in this chapter I hope to make the case that feedback can coexist with grades, and that the better we are with feedback, the more power feedback has to trump grades in terms of student learning. I show you how to preserve spaces for feedback to flourish so that it remains a powerful shaper of writers' identity and their craft. But that cheerleading aside, I confess, this has been the hardest chapter for me to write because I am deeply uncomfortable with the stronghold grading has in writing classrooms.

The reality: Most of us teach in a setting where grades have a tremendous amount of influence.

Grades are:

- An expectation on the part of the students, parents, and schools.
- A primary vehicle for communicating the performance of students in our classes.
- Powerful shapers of instruction, rather than the other way around.
- Unproven to positively impact learning for students, especially in the test-taking approach to grade gathering that prevails.
- Often based on recall of information rather than conceptual, transferrable understandings.
- Fixed, rather than dynamic, indicators of performance; not indicative of whether a learner can independently apply the learning in a new context.
- Often determiners of a self-fulfilling prophecy in learners.

Which leaves us in a pickle, right? Because the feedback we give and the grades we give can seem at odds with one another. As a profession, we've known the downsides of grading for decades but efforts to move away from grading, such as portfolio assessments, haven't managed to take hold. Alfie Kohn's research (1994; 1999; 2011) has shown that among many other negative outcomes, grades cause a disinterest in learning, a reluctance to take on challenges, and a lower quality of thinking (2011). Katherine Bomer, in *Hidden Gems* (2010), writes, "Grades create competitive, nervous, and perfectionist monsters out of the A students, and bored, rebellious, writing-haters out of the C and below students. Clearly, we want more for our writers" (p. 153).

A grade-based education system also works against teachers trying to instill a growth mindset in learners. In an Edutopia blog, Daniel Allen (2015) argues that schools have "inoculated" themselves against truly supporting a growth mindset by holding onto traditional educational practices, including the manner in which they use grades. As a parent, former student, and educator, I have experienced both the influence grades can have in the course of a person's educational journey and the highly charged, emotional response grades can manifest. Grades often become labels: "She is an A student. He is a B/C student." There is a finality to these labels that sucks growth mindset right out of the classroom. When we sit with young writers, we want them to feel open to share their writing with us, their challenges, and feel comfortable to turn to us to show them how to use their strengths to meet their challenges (Brown, 2012).

Grading Versus Feedback: What Are the Differences?

So let's start by defining both grading and feedback. First, grading. It is the letter or number given as an outcome of a particular task or expectation in a classroom. A grade is often given on a writing piece, on homework, on participation in class. Grades are theoretically based on class norms, performance in relation to other students in the class, and thus have an air of objectivity; but they are, in fact, subjective.

Grades are often assigned in percentages or letters and are averaged together with other percentages or letters into one final grade. Grades can be put into an Excel spreadsheet and the computer can compute, at the end of a period of time, a final number. We use grades to share with the students, parents, and school the level of a student's performance within a class. Even on standards-based report cards, we are indicating where a student's skill set is in terms of a set of standards. There is a tone of finality in grades. Grades do not cause learning but can be an acknowledgement of learning (Wormeli & Ferlazzo, 2014).

By contrast, feedback to a learner takes grade-level expectations into consideration, but feedback is inherently more individualistic. Put simply, it's what I say to a writer to help him grow, to further develop his skills. It's more personal than a grade, more tailored for the particular writer, and usually given *in the midst of learning*—to be applied immediately. Compared with grades, which of course are given for a product mid-term or as a final grade, feedback is more akin to an Olympic athlete's trainer, shouting coaching advice in the midst of a twirl, leap, or butterfly stroke. Similarly, I like to think of feedback as rooted in the Renaissance construct of apprenticeship. Think about it: Masters like Titian, Raphael, and others learned their craft through apprenticeships. Imagine the feedback in the midst of their learning!

Feedback for one student is rarely the same for the next student. It arises from the "brushstrokes" and emerging compositions of each writer. It can be written or oral, although the latter is the focus of this book. And, much like a Renaissance painter/apprentice, the student writer knows she is responsible to respond and act upon the feedback in order to grow. That's the beauty of it—built into the relational aspect of it, the student more readily takes suggested next steps because she knows the teacher/peer will circle back to check on her continued growth. (By contrast, whether an A+ paper on the refrigerator at home or a B– paper tucked in a drawer, the numerical feedback has no afterlife, no constructive, specific influence on the learner's ongoing performance.)

Feedback is not a quick statement like "Great job," which holds a tone of finality and grade-like labeling. Instead, feedback is loaded with language pertaining to future action (much more on this in Chapter 3). And because feedback can influence grades and how students interpret those grades, it can reside harmoniously with grades, and humanize them. Feedback is the heart and soul of strong instruction (Hattie, 2012; Hattie & Timperly, 2007).

Grading	Feedback
• The letter or number given as an outcome of a particular task or expectation in a classroom	• What we say to writers to help them, and their writing, grow
• Thought of as objective, grades are more subjective, varying from class to class, teacher to teacher	• Tailored for the particular writer to use immediately and/or in the future
• Often assigned in percentages, letters, or numbers in relation to grade-level standards	• Can be given in writing or in conversation
• Averaged together with other percentages or letters into one final grade	• It is up to the student to use the feedback (or not use it)
• Can be put into an Excel spreadsheet for a final number	• Implies there are next steps to take for continued growth
• Used to share with students, parents, and school the level of a student's performance within a class and sometimes ranking among other students	• Can be given by anyone
	• Is subjective
• Holds a tone of finality	• Can be documented to track growth and plan instructional next steps
• Grades are given by the teacher only	

Now that I have defined the differences between feedback and grading, let's take a historical view of grading writing. Surprisingly, it helps in arguing the need for more feedback instead of more grading.

One Historical Perspective of Grading and Feedback

In my research, I came upon a surprising discovery: Grading writing was not always the teacher's role. Feedback in writing, on the other hand, seems to have no specific birthplace, but *grading* does. The role of the teacher critiquing writing for grades, specifically for errors, begins to take shape around 1890, when a group of 11 Harvard professors were outnumbered by 630 students (Anson, 1989). They needed this system not only for expediency due to the disproportionate ratio of students to teachers, but also because these students were not the typical Harvard students of the day; these were a new surge of middle-class men who could afford this upper-class education. The professors' roles were plain: Correct the pieces to remove the "linguistic barbarisms" (defined as a "word or phrase not English") that came along with a lower socioeconomic class of students. In response to this grew a factory style of grading writing, outlined in the *Freshman English and Theme Correcting* booklet by C. T. Copeland and H. M. Rideout (1901). In this approach, professors were given correction codes to leave in the margins so that when the theme (writing piece) was revised, the student would correct the errors and thus improve the piece. This booklet instructs how to use these codes to give and understand the corrections and then fix up the theme. See below for an excerpt from page 10:

---

[1] **A few of the more common marks of corrections are:**

   Cst. Faulty construction.

   K. Awkward, stiff, or harsh.

   P. Fault in punctuation.

   R. Redundancy or repetition.

   S. Sentence objectionable in form.

These codes were then used to create a percentage of errors and, in turn, a grade. This grade could be improved with further revisions, though an "A" was rarely given (p. 76).

Below is an example of the grading technique. Notice how these correcting codes (and the word *trite*) were used to purge the piece of the "linguistic barbarisms." This was taken directly from the *Freshman English and Theme Correcting* booklet as an exemplar in correction.

SPECIMEN THEME 9

THE SALZKAMMERBGUT

~~The sight that greeted us~~ that July morning was very pleasant. Looking from our window⌄I could see the sun ~~with all its rays~~ clearing the mist that hung over the hills. Overhead was the clear, blue sky, with a white, <u>fleecy</u> cloud rapidly scudding over it. The fresh, bracing air, the cheerful sun, the sweet-smelling grass heavy with dew, (all the <u>splendours</u> of the morning) tended to make everyone in our party feel happy. Even the bird singing on the tree, and the curly-headed shepherd boy slowly driving along his flocks, seemed to be <u>suffused with</u> the warmth and brightness of the sun on that day.

As <u>we stepped</u> into our carriage and drove to the salt-mines we passed <u>many fields</u> with the fresh mown hay in large stacks, and in the <u>gentle breeze</u> the pleasant odor drifted upwards. The farmers drove past on their large, rumbling wagons bound for the market, which was already filled with a mass of venders disposing of their wares.

At last we arrived at the mines and soon slipped on the rubber suits and caps <u>they</u> provide <u>for you</u> there, each with a lantern in his hand <u>ready for the fray</u>. A funny looking set we were. The ladies with large bloomers and bulky coats and the gentlemen looking just as awkward.

R.

R.

Trite.

Too much.

p.

p. ??

Quite a trick!

p. Trite

Pt. of view lost.

p.

?

K.

p.

Vb.

When this approach was designed, many in education were sorely set against it. In fact, another Harvard professor, L. B. R Briggs, wrote in response to one student's writing critique: "There were a hundred things to say about the composition; and the boy, by the strong intelligence of his work, showed himself able to apply them all. Yet it was nobody's business to examine his writing minutely. Nobody had time for him" (Briggs, 1890, p. 311). A student also wrote, in response to this type of approach to writing correction, "Have I got any real good out of it? Speaking candidly . . . I do not feel that I have got very much out of it,—that I am better off than I was at the beginning of the year. In an endeavor to conform to certain rules, I have lost all originality,—everything has a sort of labored rehashing, which makes whatever I have to say dull and uninteresting" (Copeland & Rideout, 1901, p. 80). Of course, there were many others that endorsed this approach at that time.

Flash-forward a century, and we are still wrestling with this issue. Take a look at the following Edutopia blog from 2011, which mimics this same 1890s approach. It recommends that middle school teachers

> create a key of feedback symbols [to] identify the most common errors that you predict you will see . . . that you can use in the margins instead of writing in sentences or bullets. (Wolpert-Gawron, 2011)

To be fair, grading has taken many forms over the past 125 years. We have seen the birth of rubrics, performance scales, learning progressions, holistic grading, grading with checklists, the "stamp" method, check-check plus-check minus approach, contract grading, and more. I believe they all spring from a fundamental belief that grades can help improve the writing piece and future writing. What can we do, then, to recognize that yes, grading and its traditions are still present, but so is the writer? Feedback, not grades, may just be the key to unlock a writer's potential by developing the writer within and the writing along with it. Writing, after all, is an act of confidence (Shaughnessy, 1977, p. 85), and what can better shore up that confidence than effective feedback?

Designs to Help Feedback and Grading Play Nicely in the Classroom

Like it or not, in most schools, grades and feedback need to find a way to coexist. However, teachers and students are shackled to grades due to the very system of which they are a part. How can we design grading and feedback so they play nicely in the classroom? I found it daunting at first, but was inspired by Mildred Parten's (1932) stages of play as I considered some options. Parten described the development of play in children, and I find inspiration in these designs to create structures for grading and feedback to coexist in the classroom. These designs include:

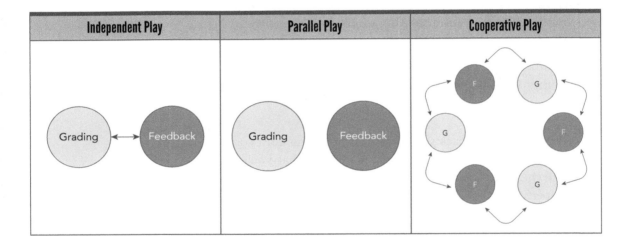

I propose that, as you (re)shape your classrooms to make space for both grading and feedback, you begin with the independent play model. Stay there, if you can, for as long as possible to keep feedback and grading separate. If you must and if your classroom trust is one in which students can separate the feedback and grading without feeling the "schizophrenia of roles," move on to the other designs in the order presented. While I have intentionally chosen this order to foster a feeling of trust, keep grades in perspective, and hold feedback sacred in the classroom, I am not implying that there needs to be growth from the design at left-first to the design at far-right. Rather, if your classroom and school require a blending of feedback and grading, I suggest moving through these designs in order. As trust in feedback increases, introduce a new design of grading and feedback if you feel it is needed. Share these designs with transparency, specifically reminding the students that the deepest intention of these designs—and all things, really—is preserving the trust that you have built for open, comfortable feedback. It is my hope that we teachers lose that feeling of a "schizophrenia of roles" as we incorporate each new design.

Design 1: Independent Play

In this case, grading and feedback will be completely independent from each other. Grading is sequestered, held in a separate place, so that none of the unwelcomed qualities of grading seep into our feedback time. In other words, separate and build boundaries around feedback time, making it a grade-free zone. We do this by first making a separate space and time for grading so students know when the conversation will be more about outcomes, criteria, and averages and when it will be about next steps, strengths, and growth. By sequestering our grading time, we preserve, the best we can in a grading world, the trust and flavor of feedback that moves writers forward.

I have done vast reading on the subject of grading, and I haven't found any consensus among experts as to the proportion of grading to feedback. I suggest that grading is at most one-eighth of the communication we have with students while the rest of our time is spent giving purposeful, writer-centered feedback so both the writer and the writing grow. Here are a few tips on how to do that.

Tips on Sequestering Grading

- Carve out time for sharing grades. Do something that marks this as grade-focused time, whether it be a simple announcement beforehand, a timer to keep it short and sweet, a shift in seating, or whatever helps adjust the environment.

- Share that you wish to nurture their writing identity in the face of grades. Share why and ask for ideas on keeping them separate and your trust intact.

- Approach giving grades in a traditional way. Hand out the graded material, ask for any questions, and then move onto writing and feedback.

- Grade just enough items to get a final grade. Ask yourself how many items this needs to be to feel confident in the grade in case you need to defend it (further suggestions on this later in the chapter).

- Make grading criteria clear and attainable. What must a student do to earn an A, B, C, etc.? Many college classes use this approach so that they can report to the school a grade and leave time for learning that is not graded (Elbow & Danielewicz, 2008).

In order to solidify feedback time, I also suggest a tool for students to collect feedback (see feedback tracker on the next page). When such a tool is in their hands, it sets up the expectation for feedback and helps everyone feel some accountability to sustaining feedback. It can act as a place for students to jot the learning from conversations with you and their peers while also acting as a place to keep track of the feedback. It keeps feedback writer-focused instead of grade-focused. If we notice the feedback tracker is empty, we give more feedback so a writer can fill it up. Instead of, or in addition to, any notes we may take, the writers can keep these notes so that they own the feedback and integrate it into their own writing, and can use it as a reference or reminder. It can serve as a reflection tool to show growth across time and the impact of feedback.

Design 2: Parallel Play

In this second design, picture for a moment the way two toddlers play; they may sit nearby in the block center, playing independently yet right next to each other, and often mimic each other's actions.

Feedback Tracker

Name:

Date: 5/18 **What I learned about myself:** I use choppy sentences. **What I learned about writing:** The sentences should flow in a writing piece. **How or when I have/can use what I learned:** I can combine sentences using a semicolon or conjunction to improve my writing.	**Date:** 5/19 **What I learned about myself:** I should strive to be more organized. **What I learned about writing:** It is important to organize my thoughts before writing. **How or when I have/can use what I learned:** Planners can help me do this. I used this when writing my literary essay.
Date: 5/20 **What I learned about myself:** I need more proof in my essay. **What I learned about writing:** Facts and quotes make your points stronger and more convincing. **How or when I have/can use what I have learned:** I used evidence in past essays to back up my claims.	**Date:** 5/23 **What I learned about myself:** **What I learned about writing:** **How or when I have/can use what I learned:**

A feedback tracker form opens up students to the power of self-reflection.

Template available for download at **http://resources.corwin.com/McGee-Feedback**

This grading/feedback design is modeled after those qualities. Grading and feedback happen next to each other in the classroom. Coexisting nicely, without sequestration, grading starts to mimic feedback.

In this design, we start with goals, and grading is focused on reaching those goals, or the effort put forth in working toward the goals. First, at the onset of a unit or writing piece or other type of writing experience, students set goals (much more on this in Chapter 5). Throughout the writing process, students receive feedback based on those goals. And, at the end of the unit, the writing is given a grade in response to the outcomes of those goals, specifically naming strengths, which are given alongside any comments or grades.

Why strengths? Grading, whether in the parallel play design or otherwise, will be most impactful to the writer's growth when it is strength-focused. As we have explored earlier in the chapter, error-focused or correction-focused grading has been a prevalent practice for over a century. Research has shown that "noticing what a student does well improves writing more than any kind or amount of correction of what he does badly, and that is especially important for the less able writers who need all of the encouragement they can get" (Diederich, 1974, p. 20). The effectiveness of this asset-based stance has been shown in research spanning decades. Ken Macrorie (1974) urges us to "encourage and encourage but never falsely" (p. 688). Strength-based response increases attendance, grades, and productivity (Hodges & Harter, 2004). Hattie and Timperley (2007) state, "Specifically, feedback is more effective when it provides information on correct rather than incorrect responses" (p. 85). Paula Denton (2015) asserts that "children build on their strengths not their weaknesses" (p. 88).

With such compelling research support, it stands to reason that feedback and grading ought to mimic each other's focus on strengths. If feedback is about setting goals, then grading will focus on the student's strengths in reaching those goals. Therefore, we may want to rethink our grading tools to include strengths. Perhaps in addition to (or instead of) checking for errors, pointing out those errors, and giving the errors our greatest attention, we can use a grading tool that focuses on strengths and allows for self-reported and teacher-reported grades. I have created one below and have a few disclaimers before using this tool. These key items must be in play for it to be effective.

1. Set writing goals that are co-created with the student and within reach, but still ambitious. Be very specific about what it means to reach the goals, with clear expectations. Write those goals down on the tool and revisit them very often, giving feedback through conferences, small-group work, and peer feedback. Keep in mind that there are anywhere from two to five goals per writing piece or unit. How to set goals and teach toward them is much more detailed in all of Chapter 5.

2. When it is time for a grade, students first grade themselves and then list the strengths—within the writing and them-selves as writers—that are evidence of meeting, or working toward, the goal. The teacher does the same.

3. Ideally, there is a conversation about these outcomes as well.

See the sample grading tool below.

Asset Based Grading Tool

Date	Goal	Writer's Grade & Comments	Teacher's Grade & Comments
5/23	Make my writing longer	I should be able to make a 5 paragraph essay easier that that I could now. 82-85	(82) You've come a long way — added a paragraph to make more of an argument, not just length.
5/23	use my grammer better	use the "and I" better. Also be able to free write the essay. 75-85	I noticed you've really worked on more complex sentences and making those fit some grammar rules. Let's explore more options together. (90)

The win–win here is the precision of supportive feedback.

Suppose the independent and parallel play designs work just fine in your classroom. No need to move into the next design, cooperative play. If you think you need more grades, you can always give more (quick) assessments during a sequestered time. Or you may give more weight to the goals or add a goal. If you feel strongly that your trust is intact with your writers, that they are keenly aware of their strengths, and that they seem comfortable moving from feedback to grading with you, consider the next design of cooperative play.

Design 3: Cooperative Play

In the design of cooperative play, it is hard to pinpoint exactly where feedback ends and grading begins. Setting up this direct relationship between feedback and grading blurs the lines between the two. As a word of caution, tread lightly here and head back to the other designs if you notice feedback is not filled with trust, comfort, and vulnerability. However, done carefully, cooperative play can create a place where feedback influences grades and grades influence feedback. There is a flow between them both, and sometimes they even overlap. Feedback, after all, can directly influence grading in a positive way. Grades, at their fullest potential, can be a source of acknowledgement for the outcomes of effort and use of feedback.

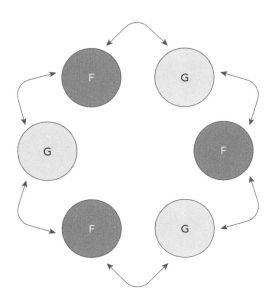

One reason cooperative play can be such a tricky design is because, as mentioned earlier in this chapter, it is hard to preserve a growth mindset in the presence of grading. Casey Bardin, supervisor of special education at Shaker High School in Latham, New York, has been working on growth mindset practices with his teachers and special education students. He shares his thinking on integrating grades and growth mindset:

> *The way we have tried to overcome being consumed with high stakes [grading] is to be transparent with students. Meaning, taking the time to explain to students that [grading] is another tool for learning. However, it still comes down to how teachers are engaging with students on a daily basis. Asking reflective questions is the best way to do this. First, am I [the teacher] including all of the components that foster a "Growth Mindset"? For example, praising the process, encouraging deferred gratification/ love of the long haul, infusion of purpose (greater good), belonging (does the student feel part of the classroom culture)? When we are constantly focusing on these questions, the by-product will be deeper learning. Simultaneously, this will result in better [grades]. Lastly, we also focus on being able to articulate how the student has made growth because on paper it may appear as a low [grade], but based on a student's perseverance it could be a huge success.*

Casey accepts that grades are a part of the school's current reality, and as a kind of counterweight, he makes it a huge priority to ensure that teachers use growth mindset approaches alongside grades. As teachers, we can help put grades in perspective and teach students how to persevere for those higher grades, especially when the grades can be a disappointment. So, in other words, feedback can be the response to grades in this design. This feedback can help repair, develop, or confirm a writer's identity. The outcome of this feedback is then, ideally, higher grades. This is a powerful place for feedback and grades to intersect.

To unpack this a little more, let's think about the essentials within this design. If the role of the teacher and the role of the student are clearly defined, this design can be much more useful in learning. After all, whether it is feedback or grading, learning is the goal!

Teacher's Role in Cooperative Play Design	Student's Role in Cooperative Play Design
• Communicates how a grade was determined • Specifically names strengths either in writing or to the writer • Maintains trust with the students through ongoing communication • Delivers feedback to help improve grades before a grade is given • Gives feedback in response to grades, especially when the grade is disappointing to the student	• Seeks out clarification on grades • Gives honest and accurate responses when self-reporting grades • Capitalizes on strengths to attain higher grades • Uses feedback from teachers and peers to improve grades • Keeps track of feedback and makes decisions on how to use the feedback

Not only is it important to clarify roles, it is also crucial to specify outcomes so that writers know what it takes to achieve particular grades. As teachers, we cannot keep the secret to attaining high grades within our own heads. We need to share our expectations (Cambourne, Handy, & Scown, 1988) so that students know what it is toward which they are striving. This can come in the form of goals or in a grading contract. Peter Elbow and Jane Danielewicz (2008) argue for the use of contracts in order to be transparent with the student, equalize the power differential in the classroom, and improve teaching and learning. Elbow and Danielewicz use their contracts in college, though they are certainly applicable from the third grade up. Inspired by Elbow and Danielewicz, I have created a contract that you may want to use with your students.

This contract can be modified in many ways. First, the wording can be made more or less sophisticated depending on the grade level. Notice it does not include much about the quality of the writing until earning an "A" grade. It can be cocreated with students or at least revised based on student input. This approach further minimizes the power differential from student to teacher. You can add or take away expectations depending on diverse learners such as special education students, English language learners, or other learning challenges. A contract is pliable and meant to suit your own classroom and writers. One contract can be used across the entire school year, or a different contract can be employed for each unit of study or writing assignment. The power of grades and feedback are then essential and intertwined with crystal-clear expectations.

Sample Grading Contract

You are guaranteed a B if you:

1. Engage in learning in class.
2. Complete all writing assignments.
3. Give thoughtful peer feedback during class.
4. Use feedback carefully, sometimes intentionally choosing not to use feedback.
5. Ask for feedback to help you reach your goals.
6. Sustain effort and investment on all writing.

To earn an A, your writing must meet and exceed the goals of the unit. (*Sample goals:* Use elaboration techniques to clearly teach your reader about your topic. Use punctuation and sentence structure to intentionally add voice.)

Another Sample Contract

You can earn a B if you:

- Use your writer's notebook as a place to collect ideas, try out new writing techniques, and make an essential part of your writing life.
- Take your writing through the writing process from idea conception through publication, working to improve your writing each and every day until the due date.
- Consider and try out feedback from all writers, including the teacher, choosing carefully the feedback that helps you meet your goals.
- Exhibit a "stick-with-it-ness" when writing becomes challenging or frustrating.

To earn an A, your writing must show growth from the start of the unit to the end, and you must be able to articulate what you learned.

It is essential to clarify the meaning of the wording in the contract so that students know exactly what your expectation is on engagement, for example. What exactly does engagement look like to you and your writers? Perhaps you define this as interaction with the learning at hand with effort and care, or maybe you have a different way of defining "engagement"? What is thoughtful feedback in your setting? Maybe specific writer-centered advice or thoughts, or perhaps a variation on that for your classroom. Whatever you choose, be sure to discuss the wording and expectations through examples and nonexamples in order to clarify and crystallize your students' understanding and use of the contract.

Performance scales can provide these crystal-clear expectations as well, especially when shared with the student long before grading. A performance scale is a set of criteria on which a student will be graded. Performance scales are not the same as rubrics, though they are often mistaken for each other. A rubric, unlike a performance scale, has a set of indicators for each criterion to show proficiency levels. They are much more detailed than performance scales. Performance scales often only require the grader to give a number in relation to the criteria. See the example on the next page.

Within a performance scale we can choose what to grade—and it does not always have to be the qualities of good writing. Notice how the tool,

Writer's Notebook Feedback and Grades

Name: _____

Date of Writer's Notebook: _____   Grade: _____

Grading Categories	What Grade I Give My Writer's Notebook	What Grade My Partner or Teacher Gives My Writer's Notebook
1. **Volume:** I have written often and as much as possible in my writer's notebook. I took risks with ideas, plans, and other types of rehearsal and experimented in my notebook.		
2. **Variety:** I have tried out different topics, ideas, and strategies, especially those that I have learned in minilessons and conferences.		
3. **Thoughtfulness:** I have written with care and dug deeply into the stories I have written.		
4. **Maintenance:** I have taken good care of my notebook, bringing it to and from class.		
Grades: 4 = Above Standards 3 = Meets Standards 2 = Approaching Standards 1 = Below Standards	**My Writing Plan:**	**Comments/Goals:**

inspired by Linda Rief and Christina Joseph, has removed the focus from writing-specific qualities and instead set up grades for effort, thinking, and responsibility. It also gives students the chance to reflect on their own growth by self-reporting grades. It makes the assumption that from these grades come plans for future work.

One disclaimer when using a performance scale: You will need to decide to be very transparent with your students exactly about what is below, approaching, meeting, and exceeding standards. This is different in each grade level and depends upon the curriculum you follow as well as the expectations in your classroom. Again, sharing examples and nonexamples of these expectations will add clarity for you and your writers.

Translating These Tools Into Different Grading Systems

Every school has a different way of approaching grading. Some schools expect a standards-based approach where students are rated on their proficiency against a particular set of standards. This is often on a 1 through 4 scale, with the 4 exceeding standards. Others report a traditional grade on an A through F scale. Even others have a percentage scale, so that an average number is the final grade. I have also seen report cards that are a hybrid of standards-based and traditional grades. These show an average for performance within that class along with where the student falls in relation to the standards. Whatever the case, all of the grading tools in this chapter can be translated into the grading system you use. It may be helpful to design what you and your school consider a conversion chart from standards-based, to percentage, to grade. I have created one as a reference on the next page.

What to Grade? A Subjective Answer to an Important Question

No matter the grading tool or the grading language (standards-based, percentage, letter grade), what matters most to grading is *what we choose to grade*. Many schools that I have worked in have already specified what must be graded by the teacher and what weights each

Conversion Chart for Grading Tools

Standards-Based	Traditional Grade	Percentage
Exceeds Standards: 4	A+	98–100
Exceeds Standards: 4	A	94–97
Exceeds Standards: 4	A–	90–93
Meets Standards: 3	B+	87–89
Meets Standards: 3	B	83–86
Meets Standards: 3	B–	80–82
Approaching Standards: 2	C+	77–79
Approaching Standards: 2	C	73–76
Approaching Standards: 2	C–	70–72
Below Standards: 1	D	65–70
Below Standards: 1	F	Below 65

of those items holds in the final grade. If you are in that setting, you probably have very little wiggle room for choosing what to grade. If you are in a setting with more freedom to choose what to grade, I offer my opinion.

If we think of grades as an opportunity to shine a light on what we value in the whole of writing and for the writer, we can design our grades based on our values. Personally, I value the work as much, if not more, than the product. I value the process of getting feedback and using it to grow and learn to meet our goals. I value risk taking and making intentional writing choices. I value reflecting on the learning process, all of the ups and downs, to hold onto new learning for future learning. Take a moment to consider your values and where they may differ from mine. You may, then, go ahead and consider what you value most and how you would like that to play out in grades. The following tools may be helpful. These are based on work from my friend, colleague, and mentor, Gravity Goldberg.

Area to Assess	How We Can Assess It	% of Final Grade
Writing Habits: The attitudes, behaviors, and actions writers take to learn and grow, including setting goals.	• Observations • Collect notebooks • Conference notes • Checklists • Performance scales • Grading contracts • Feedback trackers	25
Summative Assessments: Post-assessments, writing on-demand pieces at the end of a unit, tests, and quizzes that show us the outcomes of learning.	• Observations • Checklists • Performance scales • Rubrics • Other traditional grading approaches (i.e., number of questions correct on a test)	25
Meeting Writing Goals: Goals set for the writing piece, the writing unit, or other specific learning targets, and where the writer falls within reaching those goals.	• Reflections • Conferences • Notebooks and published pieces of writing with rubrics • Writing on-demand pieces • Grading contracts	50

When considering my values, I grouped them into three categories: writing habits, summative assessments, and meeting writing goals. I realize that these three categories overlap in places and will ultimately use the same assessments in more than one category.

Perhaps you may be wondering, where do the writing standards fall in this structure of grading? The content of the writing itself? Specifically, the "summative assessment" portion and the "meeting writing goals" portion allow space and time specifically to look at the content of the writing in terms of standards and expectations. For example, you may use a rubric to grade a writing piece in relation to the standards and unit goals in order to focus specifically on the writing content.

If you find that the above suggestions do not jive with your values, the following chart on page 50 can be helpful in determining what you will grade and what weight it will take on. Simply jot down the areas you wish to assess and then decide on how you will do so. Finally, decide how much weight you will give each area.

Wrapping It Up

The intention of this chapter is not to resolve, by any means, the debate of grades over feedback, the purpose of grades, the value of grades, or to tell you how to grade. Instead, it is meant to argue that we, as educators, have outgrown traditional, corrective grading practices as the sole form of response to writing and to share the many ways in which feedback and grading can coexist—be "integraded"—in our classrooms. It is my hope that when you use the many tools here you personalize them for your own setting and your own values to support the learners in your classroom. It is also my hope that feedback outweighs grading in great proportion and that these tools help you create the space for meaningful, powerful, writer-centered feedback.

Grading Framework

Areas to Assess	How We Can Assess Them	% of Final Grade

Chapter 3

Feedback Fundamentals

The aim is to provide feedback that is "just in time," "just for me," "just for where I am in my learning process," and "just what I need to help me move forward."

—John Hattie, *Visible Learning*, p. 137

With the opening quote from John Hattie in mind, read the following list and put a checkmark beside the feedback that you think works:

"You are an amazing writer!"

"If you put more effort in, you could be a good writer."

"Please add more details in this section here, and watch your tenses."

"Where are your paragraphs?"

"I would like this paragraph better if you indented."

"I love the way you added voice in this piece."

Yes, I know, I have asked you sort of a trick question. What Hattie would probably say is "none of the above," because a more influential way to use feedback is to customize it for the student and minimize your role as all-knowing "blesser" of writing. In this chapter, we are going to zero in on four fundamentals that will help you frame feedback well in your classroom and understand the shortcomings of comments like those above.

Effective feedback is all about the timing. That is, if it's going to have a lasting, positive effect on learning, it has to be based on a strategically timed exchange of information between the novice and the expert (Hattie & Temperley, 2007). We must first solicit and gather information from our writers, without making any assumptions or prejudgments about what we imagine they must need. We can do this in lots of ways: through conversations or conferences, through studying their writing or watching their writing work from afar, or through any other ways of first honing in on what that writer is doing, almost doing, and not yet doing. And, with this information in mind, only then deciding on the feedback that is suited for that writer, at this time.

This is not always easy work! There are many invisibles that go into designing effective feedback—intentions and decisions that can be hard to see when observing a teacher at work. If only we could get inside the mind of the teacher whose feedback always seems to be customized, spot on, and compelling! The good news is, I've done significant action research on my own feedback process and that of thousands of students and hundreds of teachers. I've distilled the invisibles into four fundamentals of feedback:

 Fundamental 1: Discover the Writer's Identity

 Fundamental 2: Set the Tone

 Fundamental 3: Use Formative Assessment

 **Fundamental 4: Deliver Feedback
That Has the Power of Three**

In this chapter, we will spend some time cracking open these fundamentals.

 ## Fundamental 1: Discover the Writer's Identity

We've talked for years in our field about the importance of the student–teacher relationship. Hattie identifies this relationship as one of the top 10 most important conditions for instruction (right next to feedback!). He describes the student-centered teacher as one who "is passionate about engaging students with what is being taught and helping them to succeed. Overall, a student-centered teacher has warmth, trust, empathy, and positive relationships." But, I've often thought, what does a "warm, trusting" relationship really mean to a writing teacher? Does that mean saying "good morning"? Using a student's name often? Smiling and being friendly? How do the best writing teachers operationalize the research on relationships to the nuances of writing?

The strongest teacher–writer relationships I have experienced and studied begin with the writers themselves, with the teacher discovering and developing the writer's identity. Let the students get the message that they possess untapped potential in learning writing. And through that belief, one of a growth mindset, every day is an opportunity for growth. Let me define what I mean by "writer's identity." To me, it's a self-concept a student has, that is comprised of current skills, curiosities, insecurities, memories, and experiences as a writer. Much like a snail carries its shell on its back, a writer has inside a shell full of interests, talents, particular likes, and dreams—and it's our job both to discover and enhance them throughout the year.

Essential to effective feedback is to *know* our young writers—who they are, what makes them tick, and how they identify their strengths and challenges. Of the four fundamentals, discovering each writer's identity is the one I hold most dear, and the one, as teachers, we need to shout about from the rooftops because it's so undervalued in American education. The heart and soul of this book rests on this fundamental, and here's why:

When I work with young writers, I am constantly amazed at just how open and aware they are of their identity—their strengths and challenges in writing—once I've invited them to let down their guard with me. In a sense, this is all I need to help them develop their writing, because when a writer possesses a positive and strong writing identity, he or she is more inclined to invest in writing with passion and engagement. The writer's identity influences every choice a writer makes, whether to invest and engage in writing, or to avoid it at all costs. Teachers can help discover this positive writing identity by first developing a positive relationship with the student. To explain this concept with more clarity, let me share the conversation I had with Max, as I worked to discover and develop his writing identity. I started out by saying, "Max, would you tell me about you as a writer?" A surprisingly simple question followed with some pretty revealing responses.

Max: I am not that good at writing.

Me: What makes you say that?

Max: I get bad grades. I don't like writing. I like free writing, though, but I don't like when teachers tell me how and what to write.

Me: Are there times you do like to write or places you write when it is not assigned?

Max: I do like to write fantasy, though, and write that all the time at home.

Me: Well, I believe that there is a writer within all of us, even if we don't feel particularly strong at it. I think you may believe that too, deep down inside, because you said you like to write fantasy, you like free writing, and you write on your own. I can identify with not feeling strong about writing— I have been there myself, and even at my age I am still trying to figure that all out. But I can help you discover that writer within you.

Max: I like fantasy writing.

Me: What do you do well in fantasy writing? We can take those strengths you have in fantasy writing and bring them to the writing that you don't have a choice in. While it may not be instantaneous, you will see that your strengths can really help you tackle the hard parts of writing. What are your strengths in writing fantasy?

Max: Humor. I like to make my stories funny.

Me: Well, your next writing piece is opinion and you can certainly use humor to be more convincing! How about we make this a goal for you . . .

As I reflected on the conversation with Max's teachers, Nancy and Jess, who had been observing, here are some things we named as important writing identity discovery moves.

- First, we noticed the space Max had to answer comfortably and freely about both his strengths and challenges in writing.

- We also agreed that sharing my own challenges and strengths with Max made him more willing to do the same.

- Nancy and Jess pointed out that I asked the student to name precisely what he felt he did well in his preferred genre, and in so doing, I in a sense "outed" his main passion, and then used this knowledge to name a next step that would be based squarely on this strength. In other words, if I'd just let it be that Max liked fantasy writing, I might have mistakenly deduced that was the whole of his writing identity. By discovering a subset passion within that—humor writing—I helped him name a more nuanced identity, and I had a fuller sense of what he'd like to be known for as a writer.

Much like a great character in fiction (not to mention any human being!), writers are a blend of sometimes harmonious and sometimes conflicting qualities and behaviors. We often demarcate those who are "poets" or "nonfiction writers" or "funny writers" in the classroom, and what I want to show you in this section, and throughout the book, is that through dialogue and feedback, we can strengthen our students' writing by discovering and developing these idiosyncratic blends sooner.

Conversation Moves to Discover the Writer's Identity	Possible Ways to Phrase Comments to Open Up Student Writer
Give space for the writer to talk comfortably and freely about both her strengths and challenges of writing	"Tell me about you as a writer." "Would you share more about that?" "What makes you say that?"
Draw out more from the writer to discover the other dimensions of this writer	"What else?" "Tell me more . . ." "I'm curious about . . ."
Share your vulnerabilities	"I can identify . . ." "I often feel the same way . . ." "I remember a time . . ."
Offer support	"Thank you for being so open." "I can help you discover . . ." "Let's imagine ways your strengths can help you meet your challenges."

How to Begin

You might begin this discovery work during the first week of school, by making a plan to meet with three or four students a day, so that within just a couple of weeks you have met with each one. I usually have a conversation first and ask questions that help me get to know them as people and as writers. I jot down as much as I can without sacrificing the conversational tone too much, just to be able to gather notes that I can refer to later. Some examples of language I often use in these conversations:

- Tell me about yourself as a writer . . . as a person.
- What do you consider your strengths as a writer? Your challenges?
- When has writing been a pleasing, positive, or important experience for you?
- Do you have a writing life outside of school?
- When are you most compelled to write?
- When have you seen your writing move others emotionally— maybe they laughed or cried or had an "aha!" moment or were moved to action?
- What have been some of the tough times in writing for you? Times you have felt a bit uneasy or defeated in writing?

What's Your Writing Identity?

Name: _____

If...	Then...	Comments
You write on your own time but mostly keep it to yourself, like a diary or personal collection of writing	You might be the type of writer who uses writing to learn both about yourself and the world around you.	
You write when you are upset or bothered about something to create change	You might be the type of writer who uses writing to change the world and solve problems.	
You write stories that are based on characters in your favorite books	You might be the type of writer who finds their greatest inspiration from other authors.	
You do all you can to avoid writing	You might be the type of writer who is still figuring out where writing fits into your life.	
You write to make others laugh	You might be the type of writer who uses humor not only to entertain but to change the way people think, feel, and act.	
Your sketch and writing seem to go hand in hand	You might be the type of writer who needs to envision their writing first and will help your reader envision clearly as well.	
You most often write informational text	You might be the type of writer who is looking to teach others about important topics.	
You write using technology (e.g., blog, Wattpad)	You might be the type of writer who keeps the audience/reader in the forefront of your writing process.	
You . . .	You might be . . .	

Some more space to tell me about you as a writer:

After these conversations I dig a little deeper in the discovery process by asking writers to jot some thoughts and ideas on a writing identity form. I take some time in class to ask students to complete this thoughtfully and then schedule brief conferences to discuss it with each student over the next week, doing several conferences a day. I try to start my year with this, and then revisit it periodically throughout the year, though you can start it at any time.

Here are one writer's responses.

(1a)

What's Your Writing Identity?

If...	Then...	Comments
You write on your own time but mostly keep it to yourself, like a diary or personal collection of writing	You might be the type of writer who uses writing learn both about yourself and the world around you.	Ehhh; sometimes.
You write when you are upset or bothered about something to create change	You might be the type of writer who uses writing to change the world and solve problems.	I don't really do that.
You write stories that are based on characters in your favorite books	You might be the type of writer who finds their greatest inspiration from other authors.	Kinda do that.
You do all you can to avoid writing	You might be the type of writer who is still figuring out where writing fits into your life.	I do not do that at all!
You write to make others laugh	You might be the type of writer who uses humor not only to entertain but to change the way people think, feel, and act.	I do that sometimes.
You sketch and writing seem to go hand in hand	You might be the type of writer who needs to envision their writing first and will help your reader envision clearly as well.	Sometimes...
You most often write informational text	You might be the type of writer who is looking to teach others about important topics.	I am not a non-fiction writer.
You write using technology (i.e. blog, wattpad)	You might be the type of writer who keeps the audience/reader in the forefront of your writing process.	I like to draft first.
You... write comic strips	You might be... Influenced to make people laugh and to be silly.	yeah! I am writing daily comic strips this moment!
You...	You might be...	

Some more space to tell me about you as a writer (you may use the back too):

I love this treasure—evidence of this young writer's multifaceted identity.

When I read this chart, I learn so much about this writer. Michael clearly loves to write, yet not nonfiction. He is a mixture of a full-on comic book writer, with a hint of writing for himself and a touch of writing to make others laugh. Knowing this about him can certainly help me see the broader picture of a writer, not just a third-grade student. And with this information, his teacher can—and has—taught him that the gifts he already possesses as a writer are the very things that will help him tackle his challenges.

A writer's identity is both complex and ever evolving, through new experiences, challenges, mistakes, moments of celebration, others' reactions, and practice. This evolution of identity correlates directly with an evolution in the writing itself. So you start with the writer's identity form, have a 5-minute conference to explore it, and then in the weeks that unfold from there, you use these initial insights almost as a pair of "reading glasses"—a lens on students' writing work—that informs your feedback and instruction. We'll keep looking at this ongoing process throughout this book, but for now, let's take a tour of one student writer so you can see what I mean about how far a student writer can range and develop when a teacher attends to the identity early on.

Morgan is a fifth grader, typical in many ways. In her first reflection, early in the school year, on her own writing identity, she identified the many complexities of herself as a writer. Note, though, the draw she has to writing narrative, fiction specifically.

Morgan's Writing Identity Evolution

Better Understanding Our Writing Identities

Morgan Rooney, age 11

Morgan is the type of writer who . . .

Morgan is the type of writer who tends to take too long in a moment, but describe it very well. She loves using the strategy show not tell, which makes it hard to speed up a moment not so important. She enjoys a comfortable spot with no distractions. Sometimes,

(Continued)

(Continued)

she gets unfocused if others are detracting. She likes writing fictional/realistic fictional stories, but does not like a minimum of work to do.

Something Morgan notices she
does as a writer . . .

She notices that her fictional/realistic fiction writing is more satisfying than her feature articles. This is good because she has a big imagination and loves looking to see the "what-ifs" in life. To add on, she notices even the least important parts in her writing are stretched out and become quite boring.

A writing risk/technique she
wants to try is . . .

Something new she wishes to try is adding symbolism to her realistic stories. She also wants to try adding more voice into her feature articles so it won't be facts, after facts, after inferences, after facts.

This will help her become a more powerful writer because . . .

In her stories, this will help her think deeper not just as a writer but a reader. A reader because in order to know where to put symbolism, she has to know where goes, she can do this while reading. It also helps her think deeper as a writer.

Here is Morgan's first writing piece from the beginning of the year, a personal narrative.

A Wish Come True

The car engine turned on.

"Finally!" I whispered to my brother, Connor. The snow outside glittered in the headlights and than fell in the dark ground. I could not wait for dinner. I sat watching the magic until my other brother Ryan nudged me hard. I gritted my teeth in pain and glared over at him.

"What do you want?" I said making it clear to sound irritated. He was clearly annoyed at my tone, he had trouble not showing it, I noted with satisfaction.

"Were you listening?" He asked all of the sudden smug. I slowly shook my head.

"Yes" I asked, uncertain why Ryan was acting this way. Uh oh. It is Christmas eve and if I am not paying attention to my parents, its coal in the stocking for me.

"Yes?" I said trying to sound calm. I want presents. But it sounds like a question. So much for being tough.

"I asked are you excited for Christmas?" Phewf! Nothing too important.

"Um . . . Of course! Mom you should know this by now! I love the family, food, fun and presents!" I was practically jumping out of my seat. Things can get me riled up. Plus, I just sat still for an hour and a half at church. I am hyper.

"I am too." She replies with a smile and faces front seat. Five minutes later we were home.

"What's that?" I ask as we get out of the car and pile into the garage. There was a note on the door.

"I call reading it" I yell out. "It says

Dear Morgan Ryan and Connor,

I dropped her off today

So she wouldn't jump out of the sleigh

Your parents said it was okay

FYI her name is Shea

Your parents said it was alright

Be sure to treat her right

I will be back later tonight

Love,

Santa"

(Continued)

(Continued)

"OMG" I scream. I shout. I jump.

"What is it?" Connor asked.

"Maybe we got another Elf on the Shelf" suggested Ryan. Wow I can't believe they don't know. We all asked for it for Christmas. Time to break the news.

"I think we got a dog!" I shout. I plow through them and open the door to the basement mudroom.

Right as I ran to my basement my heart broke there was no dog. My eyes started tearing up and I choked. I said to myself <u>why am I worried there is more rooms in this house.</u> I sprinted to my kitchen. My eyes scan the premises. I feel like a spy being chased while looking for a special treasure. I sprint to the living room almost falling because of my socks on hardwood floor.

I stopped dead. [well, not exactly. I should say I slid to a stop.] There was a wish out of my wishes, hopes and dreams. Pearly white, curly fur and huge black nose and eyes. It was a picture out of a fairy-tale book. My heart melted. Happy tears formed in my eyes. In my very living room, on the autumn, sat a beautiful puppy about a sheet of paper when streched out. You couldn't even see her tail it was wagging so hard. I had not even noticed my brothers Connor and Ryan my uncle Dave, my Dad, my Mom and my Grandma [Gammy].

"Oh my gosh!" I yell. Everyone who was there, crowded around her as she sat there with her tail wagging in her crate.

"Ouch!" I say. I stepped on something. I look down to see what I stepped on. There was a bowl that said "water" and a bowl that said "food." Underneath the bowls was a bone shaped mat.

"Mom, look! I shout. "It's her food and water!" My brothers are still speechless. My Mom opens the crate and I scoop Shea up with great difficulty. I had never held a baby dog before.

I felt happiness and grateful swell up inside. I was glad I had not given up my hope and dreams for the warm cuddly forever mine pup that had started licking my chin.

"So the saying is right." I whisper to myself. I buried my face in her fur. "Never give up."

Morgan's beautiful narrative of the moment her dream came true shows so much about her writing identity: She's a storyteller at heart, a careful chooser of dialogue, a writer who reveals intentionally and carefully the inner story of herself—the main character—someone who writes from the heart with emotion and deep feeling, and so, so much more. After this, through a new type of writing, and strategic writing instruction from her teacher, we can begin to see an evolution of Morgan's writing identity. She writes a literary essay.

Bigger Truths About Life

By Morgan Rooney

In our books we are able to interpret the hidden bigger truths in life. The title of my novel is Maniac Magee. I believe that the bigger truth about life in my text is if someone offers you something better-like help or a home, don't recline the offer thinking that it is the noble thing to do. But embrace the gift, don't take it for granted though. Jeffrey's [or Maniac's] parents died in a car crash when he was three so he never really got to know them. On top of that he got shipped to his Aunt and Uncle who despise each other but are too strict in religion to get a divorce. Then Maniac runs away from a life that could have worked out. Finally he went to live with families and people and ran and ran. This is the bigger truth that I think the author is trying to convey.

Perhaps the author was trying to convey this bigger truth. I think this because in the text, he runs away from his aunt and uncle. Chances are, if he stayed at their house, he might have had a better life and would have been healthier. Meanwhile, he ran away from home. I know this because in the text it said "And that's how the running started. Never again return to the house of two toasters. Never again to return to school." I think this connects to what the author is trying to coney because he would be an orphan unless his

(Continued)

(Continued)

aunt and uncle took him in. This act of kindness was a gift and a big responsibility. They could have easily turned him away.

Another reason why I think that the author is trying to convey that message is when he lived at the Beale's. Jeffrey decided that him staying there was to much trouble for the family that loved him so. So, like he did before Jeffrey ran away. I know this because in the text it said "The right thing was to make sure that the Beale's didn't get hurt any more." I think that Jeffrey was just trying to do the noble thing. However he might just hurt the Beales more. I know this because they all loved him very much. As you can see, I think that Jeffrey is trying to be noble.

All in all, I believe that Jerry Spinelli was trying to convey that it is okay to accept gifts even if you think they're not necessary. I noticed that Jeffrey is very independent. Perhaps Spinelli did this on purpose. As you can see, I think that the bigger truth to Maniac Magee was never be afraid to accept help.

The next unit was nonfiction writing on the westward expansion, and I have included some of Morgan's process, both notebook work and final product, as well as the "new" identity she discovered in herself. Even before I read the "new identity" I can see a change in Morgan's writing—she is not just a storyteller anymore. She writes as a sage of life's lessons and bigger truths in literature through interpretation, carefully chosen explanation, and insight. She also writes with a carefully researched and supported point of view in informational text that brings out her bold voice. This adds a new dimension to the writer who identified herself as a lover of fiction writing—a complexity of writing identity that shows that new writing experiences can layer on new identities.

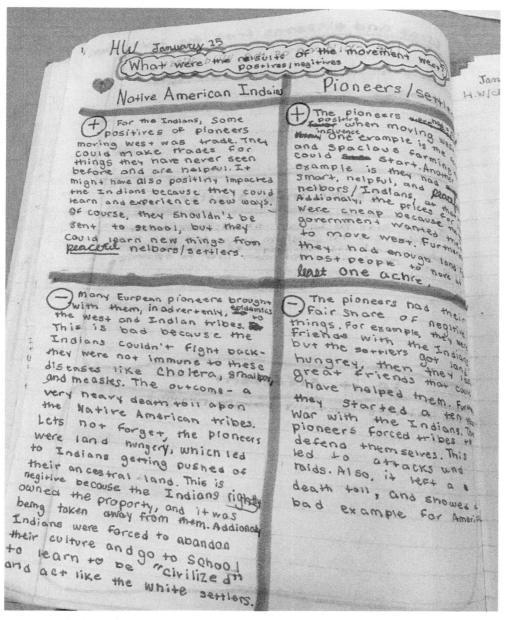

Morgan's self-chosen note-taking process to prepare for her informational piece

A Not So Perfect America

Inspired by the westward expansion of America

By Morgan Rooney

Introduction

Have you ever wondered if you were being told the truth about America's history? I mean, it seems too good to be true. Many people when talking about America's history, explain victorious battles and great freedom. Not the flaws and mistakes of the past. As a result, people see America as somewhat perfect. However, this was not always the case. When European settlers moved west, the movement disturbed Native American Indian's lives. Luckily, the Indians were helpful and peaceful to the settlers. Until broken promises and greed swept the nation-and the settlers took advantage.

Taking advantage

The trail of tears was a historic "trail" that is the tragic beaten track that the Native Americans endured during the sorrowful force out of their land. The trail of tears, however, is not a single route or geographic name. The thing is, when the Native Americans arrived from the trail of tears, the land was barren and desolated. The settlers didn't just take advantage of Indians, but stripped them of their rights and identities to.

Taking rights

After the Native American Indians were reallocated, the government and settlers figured they should do a "favor" to the Native Americans by "correcting" their personal souls. First, they shipped all the little Indian children to boarding school. Typically the boarding schools required the children to only speak english and change their name to sound American. They were forced to shed their identities and throw away their cultures and religions. Additionally, they were involuntarily enforced to practice christianism. Some people may believe that the settlers made an honest mistake and were only trying to do them a favor but in the end, the settlers stripped Indians of their identities and rights, and led Indian culture to extinction. The settlers stole the rights of the Native Americans and returned unfair treatment. Now the Indians were fighting back.

Taking charge to get it back

Meanwhile, not all tribes surrendered the land peacefully. Out the five biggest tribes, two of them rebelled back. A common claim is "Ha! See that! The Indians fought back! Who is the bad guy now?" but consider this; as much as tribal leaders opposed war, there was nothing else to do! They were suffering european diseases that they had no immunity to. They were also freezing to death and hungry. Chief Joseph (Chief Hin-mah-too-yah-lat-kekt) was a well-respected leader of some Nez Percé Indians. Tired from war he sadly spoke these words: "I am tired of fighting . . . Hear me, my Chiefs! I am tired; my heart is sick and sad. From where the sun now stands I will fight no more forever."

In the end

Without a doubt, the settlers actions were false against the Indians. In the end, the Native American culture was almost extinct. Despite the fact our country and world should be well aware of discrimination and persecution, it still is an active issue in life today. We didn't learn our lesson from this era, and we obviously didn't learn from other eras like the world war II, the civil war and other sad times. I think we can all agree the right thing to do in general would be to work out things together. Not selfishly barge into someone's life and change it forever. Would you like it if someone did that to you?

Notice how Morgan's identity has evolved. She is "now the type of person who loves to write many genres including informational." She adds: "I have grown so much more since the beginning of the year. I now am able to plan out my writing pieces, when before I didn't truly get the point of planning, which made it useless to me. I now am able to plan out my writing pieces which allows me to know what I am going to say which makes my writing powerful."

Morgan's NEW Writing Identity

Better understanding our writing identities

Morgan Rooney, age 11

I am now the type of writer who . . .

I used to be the type of writer who did not really like writing informational articles and essays at all. Meanwhile, I am now the type of person who loves to write many genres including informational. I think it is fun to come up with a fictional plot too. I make sure in my informative writing that I don't repeat my facts and come up with new ways to present them. Sometimes in my non-fiction writing I have trouble incorporating text evidence because I like to put so much of my thought in. However I know that it is very important to merge the two and keep a balance. Text evidence gives proof of your belief so I should put more in in order to keep my facts reliable. Fiction is fun because being creative is what really matters and there are no rules to your imagination.

I am now a powerful writer because . . .

I have grown so much more since the beginning of the year. I now am able to plan out my writing pieces, when before I didn't truly get the point of planning, which made it useless to me. I now am able to plan out my writing pieces which allows me to know what I am going to say which makes my writing powerful. Additionally, I am a powerful writer because I put in a lot of feeling, voice and powerful words that grab the reader's attention like <u>gullible</u> and <u>hazardous</u>. This allows the reader to think deeper and for the author (me!) to push myself to find higher-level words.

Sabian's Writing Identity Evolution

Sabian's teacher describes him: "He is a tad of a perfectionist, almost where he gets too nervous about his work. We have been working on loosening him up! He has really developed this year, though—from an anxious reader/writer to one who is willing to dive in, get messy, and make mistakes!" Look at the difference in his reflections on his writing identity. His first is slightly self-critical, yet his second shows this incredible insight into writing using the metaphors of *statue* and *clay*.

Sabian's earliest writer's identity reflection:

I am the kind of writer who . . .

I like to over elaborate my work without it being needed, leaving my response without a purpose. Lately, I have been trying to stop that by timing myself in the time expected that it should be finished. My first copy of work tends to have no understanding. As I edit, it becomes understandable. I work my hardest to do my work the best I can. I used to think I needed to write lengthy responses when really, that doesn't matter. Now I know it's the quality that counts. Once I learned that, I have been trying to create my responses with quality instead of length.

Sabian's latest writer's identity reflection:

I am now the kind of writer who . . .

Before, I used to take hours of my time to make my work perfect. Now, I am able to turn in a response without being worried about how good or bad it might

(Continued)

(Continued)

turn out to be. I realized that having a perfect response does not matter, the thought put in it is what makes it uniquely my own. One thing I tended to do in the past was make my response as if it were a statue, perfect. Now, I know that a response doesn't have to be perfect to be good. This made me think that a writing piece should act as if it were a piece of clay. For example, when playing with clay you are in charge of mold/build of it to look the way you want it to, and then when you're done you can change it. On the other hand, a statue gets built and it never changes. I think this can relate to writing because when you write a response you are in charge of what you want to make. And every response you write should be uniquely and wonderfully your own. When I came in as a writer in 5th grade I was very worried because when I went to write a response I wanted it to be perfect, nothing else. Now, I am a very confident writer.

Sierra's Writing Identity Evolution

Another example of how a writing identity evolves comes from Sierra. She says she likes to write true stories but embellish them "to make them interesting and cooler." She prefers to write for herself, however, without too many limitations. Little do we know, from this description, how nervous she was about sharing her writing. With time and lots of writing, in personal narrative, argument, and informational pieces, as well as plenty of reflection, risk taking, choice making, goal setting, and support from her teacher and fellow writers, Sierra's identity has evolved. When we hear from her in response to her "new writing identity," we see that Sierra has a newfound confidence about sharing her writing with her classmates.

Earlier in the year:

Identifying Who We Are as Writers

By Sierra Lamonte

I am the kind of writer who . . .

I like to express myself when I write and just go with the flow and not have just one set plan. I like it when I can just sit and write not having a specific assignment and just being able to free write. I'm not the best at writing for a long time I usually write until I run out of ideas. It is harder for me to be productive well I write if the room is loud or even if there is just a few people taking. I definitely do my best work when it's quiet and I'm not distracted.

Something I notice I do as a writer . . .

I like to write about real things that have happened to me but exaggerate on them to make them for interesting and cooler. I also know that I have trouble writing limits or a required amount because I usually just like to write as much as I can express not more or less because then my ideas get mixed up and changed.

A writing risk/technique I want to try is . . .

I want to try to be more expressive of my opinion and not be afraid to say what I am thinking. I will put more of my ideas in my work but I will still incorporate text evidence. I believe that will make my work more persuasive.

This will help me become a more powerful writer because . . .

I won't be scared to really put my all into my work and try my hardest to make it the best quality it can be. I think that the first step to becoming a good writer is to explore your abilities what you can do and how you can get better and that is what I'm going to do so I'm not afraid if people will think it's good or not.

Later in the year:

My New Writing Identity

I am __NOW__ the kind of writer who...

Try's to explore and do my best at whatever is being thrown my way. I won't anymore just settle for the minimum, and don't feel completely done until I push for the maximum. I enjoy taking the full journey of writing because when you think about it in the big run, you only get the chance to explore this writing piece once so why not go for it with the best of your ability.

One thing I noticed from my identity from the bigenning of the year was I said I was scared my work wouldn't be good enough so I just wouldn't share. Now I know I can feel confident because I take pride and try my hardest on all my work.

I am now a more powerful writer because...

I know I don't really have to fit a mold but I can write more freeley. I don't have to necessarily have to think about doing it right but kind of doing it how I'm cofterable.

In the beggining of the year We did a publishing partly for our personal narratives and I was very scared to share my piece. When it was my turn to share I read it quick and quietley just to get it over with. Now I found a great new confidence and excitement to share my work. I think I got it because I try my hardest on my work and know that my teachers and class our supporting me all through my learning journey no matter what.

Lily's Writing Identity Evolution

Earlier in the year:

Lily

Is the kind of writer who is capable of writing in a mannerly time, has good grammar/punctuation, and can write good dialogue. However, sometimes she tends to keep one moment a little bit too long, and lacks suspense and interest. A risk/technique she wants to try is not being afraid to take pieces out of her writing that she knows aren't really necessary. To add on, something she notices she does as a reader is sometimes take a little too much time deciding on little moments. On the other hand, she also brainstorms ideas and is good at writing down ideas before hand. She will do this by writing down in her notebook the bigger focus and ways she might write, for example, techniques and such.

Later in the year:

Lily's New Writing Identity!

I am the new type of writer who . . .

Writing is a form of creativity and your perspective of life. When you write, you express yourself, your emotions, your ups, your downs, your life. When I think of writing I don't think of the thing that I try to do a bit of everyday, but I think of what I put my time and energy towards. If I fall, I get back up. This leads me to believe that I am the type of writer who can be strong and come back stronger. I can also write words with power and make others feel something, perhaps even consider my point of view. I can also spread emotion towards the reader.

(Continued)

> (Continued)
>
> I can do this because I have determination and because I want to do this. A thing that always helps me get better and stronger is for other writers that have gone through what I have to help me and give me advice. Although they never give me answers, they give me the sugar to sweeten my batter. Writing gives me a voice to take a stand and tell others what I believe in. Writing gives me wings to open up and soar.

*   *   *

Feedback Fundamental: Set the Tone

Alejandro

Casey

Tia

http://resources.corwin.com/ McGee-Feedback

To read a QR code, you must have a smartphone or tablet with a camera. We recommend that you download a QR code reader app that is made specifically for your phone or tablet brand.

These writing samples and reflections show the growth of both the writing across the year and the writer's identity. They are tied together on the journey of growth, and develop in relation to one another. If we are looking for the writing to improve by leaps and bounds, we must also, simultaneously and inexplicably, nurture the writer's identity. As the first feedback fundamental, discovering and building the writer's identity cannot be underrated. Throughout the rest of this book, we will explore the feedback you might use that has the dual purpose of developing writers' identities and also the writing itself. Before we go there, the second fundamental begs our attention and is one of the most helpful tools in discovering and building a writer's identity.

Fundamental 2: Set the Tone

The tone of feedback can enrich or spoil the feedback experience for our writers. It's that simple. In fact, the words you speak may mean nothing without the right tone. Although tone is one of those things that is hard to define, it is my Fundamental 2 for good reason! I know effective tone when I hear it, see it, or feel it, and I am guessing you do as well. The sections that follow describe some of the key tenets of establishing an effective tone with your learners; to view video footage of effective tone in action, use the QR codes that appear in the left margin and on the companion website at **http://resources.corwin.com/McGee-Feedback**.

Think about your own self as a learner. If someone says something in a tone that is rushed, sarcastic, bored, frustrated, or otherwise negative it can make you raise the barricades to protect yourself from the feedback headed your way, right? On the other hand, tone that is warm, interested, concerned, invested, or otherwise positive opens up your heart and head to feedback.

I have experienced the same with student writers. If I am giving feedback and I am not 100% present and invested, my feedback is not nearly as well received. On the flip side, even if I cannot find just the right words, as long as my tone is warm and invested, I find my feedback is more welcomed. Remember the conference I referenced above with Max? The tone was open, warm, comfortable, and an important factor in how I was able to discover his writing identity.

Although there is no agreed-upon definition of tone that is universally accepted in terms of education, I've developed a working definition to use in my work with writers: Tone is the quality, manner, or style one uses when eliciting and giving feedback.

When we consider tone, we understand it can go either way—it can be useful or detrimental. It can nurture or impair a relationship. Words alone cannot convey tone—it is the sound of the words, the language of the body, the smallest gestures, the tiniest look in one's eye. All of these qualities blend to create tone.

Since tone seems to be this invisible yet powerful quality, seemingly unexplored, I decided to do some informal research on it with colleagues. We wanted to be able to name what qualities create a tone that supports a writer's identity and helps the writer strengthen his or her writing. We set ourselves up with an inquiry: What qualities describe the tone of an impactful conference? What was important to establish that tone?

Let's visit Max's conference once again to notice the tone. I realize a transcript is not the ideal vehicle for sharing tone, so let me set the scene a bit more to help you envision the conversation. Perhaps you will read this with the same questions we did: What qualities describe the tone of the conference? What was important to establish the tone?

I start by asking Max if I could join him so we could work together. He agrees, and I smile and thank him for the time. We chat for a moment about something other than writing. And then I simply ask him to tell me about himself as a writer.

Max: I am not that good at writing.

Me: What makes you say that?

Max: I get bad grades. I don't like writing. I like free writing, though, but I don't like when teachers tell me how and what to write. I do like to write fantasy, though, and do that all the time at home.

Me: Well, I believe that there is a writer within all of us, even if we don't feel particularly strong at it. I think you may believe that too, deep down inside, because you said you like to write fantasy, you like free writing, and you write on your own. I can identify with not feeling strong about writing— I have been there myself, and even at my age I am still trying to figure that all out. But I can help you discover that writer within you.

Max: I like fantasy writing.

Me: What do you do well in fantasy writing? We can take those strengths you have in fantasy writing and bring them to the writing that you don't have a choice in. While it may not be instantaneous, you will see that your strengths can really help you tackle the hard parts of writing. What are your strengths in writing fantasy?

Max: Humor. I like to make my stories funny.

Me: Well, your next writing piece is opinion and you can certainly use humor to be more convincing! How about we make this a goal for you . . .

Max: Sure sounds good. I think it should be that I should use humor in my next writing piece. Not sure how to say that, though.

Me: How about I give you some words for that? (I jot down the goal on a sticky note and give it to him.) How does this sound? "To use humor to be more convincing in my opinion piece."

Max: I like it. And I don't stay focused when I am supposed to be writing. I have to work on that too.

Me: Oh! Okay, sounds like we need two goals, then. Let's also write a goal so you can work on staying focused longer.

Max: I like to get up a lot. And talk to people a lot. And sometimes I don't write as much as I should.

Me: All right, that is another important thing to work on. How about you jot those goals down, one on each page, and start coming up with a few ways you can meet those goals?

Max: Sure. I already know a bunch of things I can do to stay more focused on my writing. (He starts to write these down.)

Me: What we did here was important work. You opened up with me to look at your strengths and struggles, and I am grateful for that. From that we planned writing goals that you and your teacher will spend a whole lot more time discussing. Know that what we did here is not just for writing. You can use your strengths to set goals for anything you want to do.

My colleagues and I reflected on transcripts with Max and 20 other students. We looked at them as we tried to answer our inquiry questions (*What qualities describe the tone of the conference? What was important to establish the tone?*). After much discussion, we came up with a list of five qualities of tone that lead to optimal feedback and learning. I encourage you to keep these in mind in your own practice.

Five Qualities of Tone for Effective Feedback

Acceptance: When we sit side by side with a young writer and, through our tone, share that we accept them for who they are, their strengths and challenges, the learner feels free from judgment. When hearing a tone of acceptance, writers are more apt to feel comfortable sharing, and as a result, we will receive information from them to design our feedback.

© Rick Harrington Photography

When teachers use a patient, admiring tone, students adopt it too when they give peers feedback.

In Max's conference, the tone of acceptance made Max feel comfortable enough to share that he did not feel like he was a strong writer. This gave us the opportunity to take the next steps of goal setting. I tried to set that tone by sitting side by side as though we were a team working together. I smiled, nodded, listened, and let Max lead the conversation. All of this, the teachers and I believe, set the tone of acceptance.

Patience: Every teacher needs patience because coaching writing can be frustrating, and developing writing can be vexing for the writer. When our tone communicates patience, it helps everyone work through the frustration. Being patient is also a powerful way to model growth mindset thinking, because it demonstrates for the learner that roadblocks and mistakes are not "bad" but just challenges that take time to work through. By contrast, a tone of impatience is often a form of anger and can easily shut down a writer. Patience helps writers move through the sticky parts.

One thing that was not evident in the transcript on the previous pages was that Max was distracted. He looked around a lot and seemed disengaged at times. You may also have noticed the conversation seemed to have wrapped up around the first goal, and Max jumped in with another and ways to meet that goal. An impatient response might have been, "If you know how to stay focused on your writing, why don't you?" Because of patience, Max took the lead in the conversation and ended up with two important goals.

Admiration: When we admire, we look at something with wonder and awe (Goldberg, 2015). We admire through many different lenses to see more clearly the gifts and strengths of a writer. We can acknowledge the writer's gifts and strengths—so very often young writers are not aware of these strengths or how to use them.

This was exactly the case with Max. He was certainly open to sharing his strengths, and could identify them readily, but he was quite surprised to learn that he could use those strengths in writing something other than fantasy. With this as a goal, he was now more invested than before our conversation. Admiring his strengths led us to this opportunity.

Openness: When we approach a conversation with a tone of being okay with whatever may come, we take an important step in making the feedback about the student, not about ourselves. Feedback for students starts with the students first. And through the openness of listening, we discover things we may or may not have expected.

Gratitude: When we show a disposition of appreciation for a writer's attempts to write, for their gifts and challenges, for their efforts and decisions, we look at both the writing and the writer in a precious way. When there is a tone of gratitude, there is also a feeling of acknowledgement of what has been done. Appreciation in the face of struggle is also a strong way of acknowledging and using a growth mindset—we show appreciation for the hard parts, mistakes, and difficulties because this is where learning happens.

Gratitude was evident at the end of the conversation when I thanked Max for opening up. That, my colleagues thought, acknowledged the willingness to share struggles so that hopefully Max will be that open again in the future. It also made us, as teachers, feel thankful for the time and learning about Max that he offered. We learned much about him and also about our teaching. The biggest learning: *Feedback is first about listening.*

Establish a Listening Tone

Listening cannot be underestimated. All five of the qualities of effective tone—acceptance, patience, admiration, openness, and gratitude—boil down to listening first, next, and throughout. I have not once regretted listening to a student before giving feedback, though I have regretted offering feedback before listening! Listening means we stop talking for a moment, we put our own expectations to the side, and we let the student talk. We may listen more deeply by asking clarifying questions. By listening we equip ourselves with plenty of information to design effective feedback. We can set a listening tone through our words, actions, and reactions.

For me, listening is harder than talking. I need a few go-to phrases and reminders to help me maintain that listening tone in my words, actions, and reactions. I have collected a few here that I find useful when setting a listening tone.

In our words	"Tell me about . . ." "Would you share . . . ?" "I am interested in hearing . . ." "I am curious about . . ." "I'm listening . . ."
In our actions	Sit side by side. Make eye contact. Put the writing in between. Nod. React with honesty—laugh, sigh, pause.
In our reactions	"Would you tell me more about . . . ?" "Wait, did you just say?" "So are you saying . . . ?" (paraphrase) "Say more about that." "I am confused . . ."

Maintaining a Listening Tone When Adding a Focus

Sometimes we want to be even more focused on what we intend to give feedback on. Sitting and gathering information from a student without a clear-cut focus serves its purpose, yet at other times we need to find out more about specific writing choices or struggles. While having a focus does not stand in the way of being open to listening, doing both requires a delicate balance. We want to be sure we are supporting students with important choices and next steps, yet we want our writers to be able to express themselves openly and know we are hearing them. I find this challenging. I put together some wording (see the next page) that helps me, sort of like a cheat-sheet, for those more focused feedback junctures. I anticipated a few of the common conversations and included wording that I have heard teachers use that really seem to fit the tone of listening.

Language That Fosters a Supportive Tone

Focus	Phrases That Help the Writer Be Open to Feedback	Follow-Up Phrases to Invite the Writer to Select a Strategic Option
Generating ideas	"Tell me about some of the ideas you were working on." "How were you able to come up with those?" "How have you been working on these ideas?" "What else do you imagine doing?" "What else?"	"Something I have tried that you may want to try . . ." "Something you mentioned made me think about . . ." "Let's study this together and see . . ."
Choosing how to structure writing	"Tell me about your ideas and how you plan on structuring them." "What are the structures you may try out? What are some others?" "How is the structure supporting your greater purpose?"	"Some other structures you may be interested in . . ." "I use this structure when . . . and this structure when . . . Which will work for your writing?"
Making the most of writing time	"What's been challenging for you in writing all you can?" "What do you find works best in writing for as long as you can?" "What do you need in place to do your best writing?"	"Sometimes that happens to me and here's what I do . . ." "I know another student who has worked through similar challenges. Let's talk to . . ." "Here's what I need to do my best writing . . ."
Choosing how to publish	"Who is your main audience for this piece? How would they most likely want to hear it?" "What technologies have you seen used with this type of writing?" "In what ways do you hope to impact others with this writing?"	"I've noticed that audience often reads _____. Let's see how that will work." "Some technologies I have seen used are . . . Let's check a few of those out and see what fits best." "We can choose multiple platforms to fit different audiences. Let's imagine a few."

 Available for download at **http://resources.corwin.com/McGee-Feedback**

Why So Many Suggestions for Teacher Wording?

Many of the tools I shared in this section on tone come from conversations I have heard between teachers and students. I am intentionally sharing wording not because I believe that teachers cannot uncover their own, but because research has shown that most of us give feedback as praise or paired with praise (Hattie, 2012). We know, from earlier in the chapter, that this praise is the least useful form of feedback. So, to replace the habit of praising, we simply need to find other wording. My intention is, with the many tools in this section, that we move from praise wording to feedback wording, instantly making our feedback that much more effective.

 ## Fundamental 3: Use Formative Assessment

Formative assessment, one of those terms often tossed around in education, is worth defining here, in relation to feedback. P. D. Pearson keeps it simple: "Formative assessment is responsive teaching." James Popham calls it "a planned process in which assessment-elicited evidence of students' status is used by teachers to adjust their ongoing instructional procedures or by students to adjust their current learning tactics" (2008). In other words, formative assessment is the work we do as teachers to gather evidence about students' learning to tailor our teaching accordingly. It is powerful work! An analysis of thousands of studies of formative assessment have concluded that effectively using formative assessment can essentially double the rate of student learning, no matter the instructional approach (Popham, 2011). What's more, feedback cannot be effective without it. In order to choose the type of feedback we give, we must know where students are in terms of their learning, down to very specific details, and use that knowledge to customize our feedback.

Surprisingly, I have noticed that many teachers use ongoing formative assessment without even realizing it. If you are focusing on the writer, and eliciting information, data, or feedback from them, you are engaging in formative assessment. In other words, if you look at what writers are doing and make instructional decisions based on what you see, you are using formative assessment. Indeed, it is that simple, and yet it can also become more sophisticated and impactful

Tips for Goal-Centered Conferring and Structuring Feedback Time

A Common Conference Structure	Suggested Phrases (you will never use everything here)
Ask about writer's goal(s) (first 1–2 minutes)	"What is the goal you are working on?" "What progress have you made?" "What has been challenging?" "Would you show me where you . . . ?" "What's your larger intention in writing?" "What investments have you made?"
Name what is working in reaching that goal (1 minute)	"What I am noticing is . . ." "Ways that I see you reaching your goal are . . ." "What seems to be working is . . ." "The steps I see you took are . . ."
Suggest next steps toward that goal (1–2 minutes)	"Some next steps are . . ." "You are ready for . . ." "I imagine where you could go next is . . ." "At this point you may want to try . . ."
Optional: Model those next steps (1–2 minutes)	"Here's what that can look like . . ." "Watch me as I . . ." "Here's a quick how-to . . ."
Optional: Coach (1–2 minutes)	"Want to give it a whirl? I'll stick with you while you do." "Talk through what you are imagining . . ." "What are you going to try first? And then?" [or maybe whisper in as the student writes with quick comments of encouragement and advice]

 Available for download at **http://resources.corwin.com/McGee-Feedback**

when done intentionally. Let's explore formative assessment's details to make it even more practical when designing feedback.

First, to be clear, summative assessment and formative assessment are quite different. In Chapter 2 we talked about the difference between grades and feedback. Those grades are a form of summative assessment—once given, specifically on a report card, the assessment process is over. This is usually a grade on a test, a rubric, a performance scale, or other similar grading tools. Formative assessment, on the other hand, expects that the teacher takes the information he or she learned about the student(s) and uses it to design instruction. I feel strongly, as do others (Black & Wiliam 2001; Miller 2011; Popham 2011), that formative assessment is rarely used for grading purposes. If we compare these two forms of assessment to punctuation, summative assessment is like a period while formative assessment is like an ellipse. A period marks the end of something, where an ellipse suggests there is more to follow. Feedback needs formative assessment more than it does summative assessment.

To paint a clearer picture of what formative assessment can look like in writing, I'd like to share my first few moments with Malaky, an eighth grader. First, I admired (Goldberg, 2015) Malaky from afar. I noticed his writerly actions and choices—he sat with his head close to the paper, pencil in hand, scratching out word after word, about five or six words in all. I then took a seat next to him and glanced over his writing. I noticed each word he crossed out was the same: *then*. I asked him, "What are you revising here, Malaky? Would you share what you are thinking about and doing?" He paused from his work and shared, "I realize that practically every sentence I have written here sounds almost the same. I begin with the word *then* and then tell what happened. It sounds repetitive and I want to change it up a bit."

At this point I could have jumped in and offered some ways of mixing up the sentence structure. Instead, I chose to gather a little more information. I looked at his sentence structure a little more closely and noticed that all of his sentences were simple sentences. I also asked him, "What do you want the reader to think or feel? This can help you choose ways to revise sentences." To this Malaky responded,

"This story I am telling is really funny, but I don't think it is coming off that way." He was right. His story was hard to follow and the humor was hard to find. With this information in mind, I decided to teach a bit about setting up humor in a story, with a "punchline" sort of structure. I chose to do this because, from the information I gathered about Malaky and his writing, work on sentence structure was not the support he needed at the moment. Perhaps a little down the road, but in this case, sentence structure was not going to help him make this story clear and funny.

By spending a moment to formatively assess not just the writing but also the writer's intent, I was able to make a more careful and customized teaching decision. Here is the process I usually follow. The first three steps are where I am formatively assessing; the last two steps are what I do to teach after I formatively assess.

There are a few important moves that made formative assessment practical and student-centered:

1. Observing, or admiring (Goldberg, 2015), from afar to gather information about the writer.

2. Gathering information without judgment and as objectively as possible, without acting on assumptions or on what that day's lesson happened to be.

3. Looking for what that writer needs right now.

4. Taking a look at student writing and following up with some conversation and questions.

5. Sitting with a student and asking her about her writing, her process, and herself as a writer.

Helpful Language for Formative Assessment

- The goals you are focusing on are _____. Would you share what is working and what's been tricky?

- Tell me about what you most want in your writing. How is that going?

- Who is your audience, and what are you trying to get them to think/feel/learn?

- What is taking up your attention right now in your writing? Tell me more about that . . .

- What is it you are working on? How can I support you?

Following this process day after day, student after student, can have a powerful impact on writers and their writing. It also may be challenging as a teacher to keep all that assessment information straight and use it to preplan. You may want to consider keeping formative assessment notes. Following is a sample of these notes across the first 10 days of an opinion writing unit from Pam Koutrakos about her third-grade student, Lindsay.

Each day includes notes on her formative assessment using different sources such as a pre-unit writing sample, a conference, a notebook check, and small-group work.

Pam notices what Lindsay is doing, almost doing, and not yet doing, and includes that information in both the "+" area and the next steps box.

Pam includes what she taught Lindsay (TP stands for teaching point) so she can check in on this progress during her next opportunity for formative assessment.

Pam also keeps notes on the progress toward the goal.

NAME: Lindsay		UNIT: Opinion unit
STUDENT GOALS: Transitions to help writing flow		
TEACHER GOALS: ★ Elaboration ★		
DATE: 12/1 writing sample	RESEARCH: preassessment + Includes opening, 1 body TP, closing, reasons aligned TP: to big idea	NEXT STEPS: ★ Elaboration Study Group ★
DATE: 12/9 conference	RESEARCH: + wrote long & strong, kept to one topic. TP: when re-reading entries, think, "what big ideas do I have about this topic?"	NEXT STEPS: Boxes & bullets to organize thinking and leave space for lots of evidence.
DATE: 12/11 notebook check	RESEARCH: notebook check in entries all focused on one topic - saying same reason over & + over using different words. TP: opinion writers make their ideas truly separate by thinking "what is another, different, reason to prove my point?"	NEXT STEPS: ★ "Bullets" strategy group ★
DATE: 12/12 strategy group	RESEARCH: Elaboration S.G. ★ one way we can set + ourselves up for success is to make sure each bullet point is TP: ① aligned to topic/big idea ② truly separate from each other	NEXT STEPS: ++ Did very well! able to go back & change reasons; create distinct bullets

To put these notes in context, Lindsay wrote a personal essay about her adoration of fudge. She chose that topic herself from a few different, self-generated ideas as part of a unit of study on opinion writing. My favorite part, the closing, said, "I adore fudge. Fudge comes in so many different flavors. That's why I say, after reading this essay, you should go out and get some fudge to eat. Carrie Underwood once said, 'sometimes a girl's gotta have some chocolate' and I totally agree with that!"

Notice how tailored Pam's teaching was, according to her notes, and how student-focused her formative assessment is. We can infer from Pam's notes that Lindsay's learning progressed across the 2 weeks of feedback and the feedback matched that progression closely. So, as you work to strengthen the feedback fundamental of formative assessment, following are some pointers so that you may find success similar to Pam's.

Pointers for Formative Assessment

- Help students to set goals and assess progress toward those goals (see Chapter 5 for goal setting).

- Hold off from grading and simply gather information through studying writing, admiring the student from afar, and talking to the student.

- Jot down what you notice writers doing, almost doing, and not yet doing to help plan next steps.

- Formatively assess often, ideally 4 times a week or more, to check in on where they are in their learning. Not every moment of formative assessment is followed with feedback from you. You can decide when. I find it best to offer feedback about 2–3 times per week. These are often 2–3 minutes of feedback (see Chapter 4 on structures of efficient feedback).

- Jot down both the information you gathered and the feedback you gave and what the writer was able to do with that feedback.

Once we have a handle on where our students are and what sort of feedback we can offer them, it is time to consider the next feedback fundamental: choosing and using the right type of feedback.

Fundamental 4: Deliver Feedback That Has the Power of Three

As we explore the fundamentals of feedback, it is important to continue to dig into the specifics of feedback. Not all feedback is built alike, and the impact of different types of feedback can vary. Let's take a moment to explore the feedback that research has proven impactful and also take a look at the feedback that is not as useful.

Our feedback always includes these three attributes and steadfastly remains:

1. writing (or writer) focused,

2. based on goals or intentions, and

3. explicit in naming strengths and next steps.

Let's try it out with a writing sample from Zack. Notice that by looking at a piece of student writing, we are addressing the first attribute of effective feedback—**writing-focused**. Now, let's imagine that Zack's goal was to use text evidence to be more convincing. We would keep that in mind as we read his piece and look out for convincing text evidence, and therefore be **basing our feedback on goals or intentions**.

Harry Potter
Book Review

Rating: ★★★★★ five stars!

JK Rowling is a pionner. She made the first, as I like to call it, "special kid" series. Basicly, she made the idea of a regular kid having super awesome powers. The daringness of pioneering a genre, for goodness sake, is just amazing. Second, the realness of the whole book ties right in with our world. The wizard takes in "muggle" things is quirky and comical. Also, this book series has way more plot twists than a usual book, but just enough to make it unique.

These are just a few things the series blends into its mix. But even how good a book is that has "move over, Harry Potter" on the back, I say, Harry "aint goin' nowhere"!

As I read this piece, I notice that Zack has not used text evidence much to make his case. He does, however, set up the use of text evidence with a solid reason to back up his claim. For example, when Zack writes, "Also, this book series has way more plot twists than a usual book, but just enough to make it unique," I can imagine a piece of text evidence following this statement. So my feedback may sound like:

> **I name a strength:** *Zack, as I think about your goal of adding text evidence, I have a few thoughts. First, I notice that you have a strong way of setting up text evidence by listing out the reasons to prove your claim of "J. K. Rowling is a pioneer." Because you listed your reasons so clearly, you are ready to pull in some specific text evidence. Let me show you how.*

> **And next steps:** *There are a few steps I take when including text evidence. First, I read one of my reasons I wrote to back up my claim. Next, I think, "What part of the book can help me prove or explain this reason?" After that I go back into the book and reread that part. Finally, I either summarize or quote that part directly right after my reason.*

> *Now, you try, Zack. Let's walk through these steps together.*

Notice that this feedback includes both the strengths—what is working—and the next steps to meet the goal. No, not every experience giving feedback is that simple and straightforward (see Chapter 5 for more complex examples). Nevertheless, we strive to use writing-focused, strength-based, goal-centered feedback as often as we can. Sometimes, however, feedback may still not have the impact we are hoping for unless the writer is feeling open and comfortable about receiving this feedback.

© Rick Harrington Photography

Wrapping It Up

Most of all, no matter the setting, it is important that the four fundamentals are an integral part of all writing feedback we give. Without knowledge of the writer's identity, just the right tone, formative assessment, the feedback that has the power of three, our feedback can fall short. It is a constant area of growth for me, and I hope that as you explore the many resources that follow, you hold with you the fundamentals of feedback.

Words and Ways to
Transform Writers and Writing

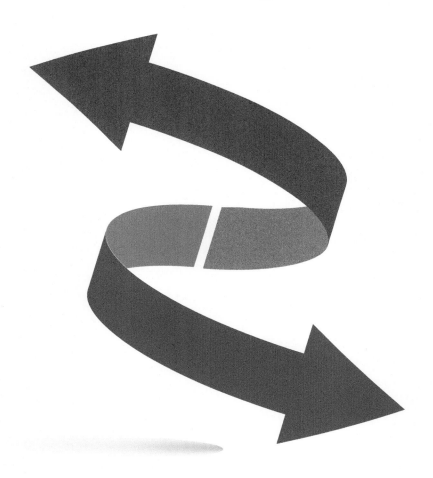

Part 2

Chapter 4

When Writers Are Stuck
Feedback to Support Risk Taking

Children have an extraordinary capacity for innovation.

—Ken Robinson's comments from his TED talk (2006)

Perhaps the toughest part of supporting writers comes when it seems like they are just not doing anything at all. There is, I believe, a common thread among all "stuck" students: Writing requires vulnerability, and stuck writers let their fear stop them. This state is deeply uncomfortable for many of our writers because it is laying open one's self. To put our ideas out there, whether stories, deep-rooted opinions, or content-area writing, can be scary. Even in relatively supportive school cultures, students may harbor insecurities of how they measure up against peers. *Are my ideas good? What about my spelling? Am I boring? Will they laugh at me if I write that I actually love playing piano or cried when my grandpa died? Will this social studies report show I am not smart enough?* In other words, there is a level of shame associated with taking imperfect action in writing. Putting words on a page is so darn *public*, right? For our students, with that endless tape of self-doubt running through their heads, writing can seem to document all they don't know rather than all they know, all they aren't rather than all they are.

Yet author, social worker, and research professor Brené Brown (2012), who spent a decade studying vulnerability, reminds us that in order for creativity and innovation to flourish, we must allow ourselves to be vulnerable: "Vulnerability is the birthplace of innovation, creativity, and change. . . . It is uncertainty, risk, and emotional exposure. It is not weakness." If fear of vulnerability is the common thread for all stuck writers, what can we do as teachers to support writing despite discomfort? This chapter is chock full of tools, conversations, and examples of ways to support risk taking despite the discomfort. Before we get there, let's spend some time digging into the concept of risk taking and its implications for our teaching.

Many have the impression that writing is a magical creation—the writer thinks for a moment, lands a pencil on paper, and *voilà!* a lovely, completed piece for all to admire. In actuality, most writers agree that the process is quite different: More often than not, it requires writers to push themselves outside of their comfort zone and try something new. For most, writing is challenging, confusing, complex, and intimidating, while at the same time life-changing, inspiring, creative, and fulfilling. We must, as teachers, share this side of writing—that writing requires risk taking as well as effort, work, revision, false starts, and phenomenal *aha!* moments.

The Iceberg Illusion: The Bulk of the Writer's Work Is Beneath the Surface

As we delve into this concept of students feeling stuck, let's first explore what writing *really* requires behind the scenes, much of which can be difficult to navigate, leaves writers gridlocked, and requires certain mindframes. Sylvia Duckworth's *Iceberg Illusion* illustrates these mindframes well. The final writing piece—what others see—is only the tip of the iceberg and may look like it was created by magic. In actuality, what really goes into creating a strong piece of writing is hard work, good habits, disappointment, sacrifice, and persistence—all worked through by a writer with a strong writing identity.

The cool thing is (pun intended), icebergs form a lot like the ways pieces of writing take shape, and it's a great analogy to share with students. An iceberg begins as part of a glacier, which forms on land and then begins to "flow and creep under [its] own weight like a viscous fluid. When the edge of the glacier advances into the ocean, the pieces that break off are what we call icebergs" (iceberg canada.com, 2016). The glacier itself first forms as an accumulation of snow, building over time. Likewise, the writing process is an accumulation of ideas, efforts, and emotions, and it is often slow, like the glacier's formation. Writing collects like snow, gathering and solidifying, growing, perhaps in a notebook, and at the right time, when it has moved off the edge, so to speak, a piece breaks off, and evolves into the final piece—the iceberg, if you will. And like an iceberg, that final writing piece is buoyed up above the water by the underwater mindframes. Without them, the piece would not emerge above the water. Without what lies beneath, the writing would sink.

Mindframe: A mental attitude or outlook. (*Merriam-Webster's Collegiate Dictionary,* 2016)

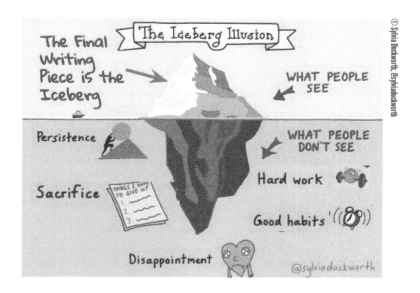
© Sylvia Duckworth, @sylviaduckworth

Underwater Mindframes: Ideas and Language to Share With Students

Underwater Mindframe	What You Might Say to Writers
Hard work: Putting in effort to make writing the best it can be. This often includes pushing yourself to do more than what is comfortable, spending more time to smooth out the writing, revising again and again, especially when you don't feel like it.	"Remember that hard work is not easy work. That is why it is called hard. Expect hard. Perhaps if it all feels too easy, you can push yourself to work harder." "Remember that hard work always, always pays off for you in the long run." "Set goals and work to meet them. Even if you don't feel like it. You will surprise yourself."
Good habits: These are the "healthy" choices we make as writers like writing every day, making the most of our time, setting goals, taking risks, and reading like a writer. Often, when a habit is a habit, it no longer feels like hard work; it just is something you do every time you write.	"Pick one habit you know will benefit you the most. Vow to do it every day." "Good habits are often planned, so you don't have to think about them too hard. Examples of good habits: Every day, have your materials ready before sitting down. Every day, pause periodically to revise a section of your writing." "Write every day. Talk to another writer every day about writing."
Disappointment: In writing, sometimes things don't work out as planned. Disappointment may come from a small mistake or something big. Both are treasures for a learner and writer!	"Sit with disappointment. Don't try to pretend it is not a feeling." "Disappointment sometimes feels terrible, but is like eating a really healthy, not very tasty vegetable. It helps us grow. Name the changes you plan on making because of this disappointment." "Think, 'This is disappointing now, but not forever.'" "Talk to others who have experienced disappointment and ask what they did with it. Try out their advice."
Sacrifice: Writers often give up some things that they may want really badly in order to make the time and give the effort for strong writing.	"We all give up something to get something. Think of sacrifice as an investment." "Imagine all you will gain. Know that what we do now, while challenging, disappointing, or hard, will be worth the work and feeling for much, much longer."
Persistence: This is a mental commitment to stay the course and stick with writing even when things get tough.	"Make a commitment to yourself before you begin that you will stick with it, no matter what comes. When you don't feel like doing something, get up, grab all of your materials, and find a different spot to work. Often, a change of location is motivating." "Make a commitment to yourself, or a friend, that you are going to do something. Follow up with yourself or your friend to celebrate what you have done." "Ignore the voices (inside your head and out) that encourage you to give up. Talk back to them and say, 'I'm not listening!'"

 Available for download at **http://resources.corwin.com/McGee-Feedback**

I believe it is important not only to share these underwater mind-frames with writers, but also to nurture and help strengthen the skills to work through the challenges these often unromantic, uncelebrated mindframes pose. Once aware of this underwater work, students might be more likely to commit to writing, find comfort in the discomfort, and take greater, more ambitious risks. We can teach writers both to expect to use these mindframes and to equip them with language that will help them work through the ups and down of "underwater" work to shore up the iceberg.

To see how you might use these underwater mindframes as a reflection tool, flip to Chapter 7.

Another important reason for supporting writers as they navigate the underwater mindframes is to bolster their identities as writers. 👓 Sometimes, writers believe they are not strong simply because they only see other peers' and published authors' tip-of-the-iceberg/final writing pieces. Little do they know, or have seen, the work that goes on to float that writing! While some writers make it look easy, it is often because they are at ease with the underwater mindframes. In fact, they find joy in these mindframes, knowing that this is the work of writers. In other words, they have a growth mindset writing identity—one that we want all writers to have. We can support and nurture this identity through a focus, and even a celebration, of the underwater mindframes.

Finally, these commitments to support and work with the underwater mindframes can allow students the permission and comfort to make themselves vulnerable so they can truly find the joy that comes with creativity and innovation in their writing. I realize that by reading a book, it can be hard to picture how all of this plays out in a classroom. Words on a page are often difficult to translate into moments in the classroom. The rest of this chapter will share tools for you to support your writers, through feedback, as they put themselves in a place of vulnerability and embrace risk taking as a tool for getting "unstuck."

Risk Taking: How Students See It

Taking risks is an essential act to learn and grow. One student I worked with described it as "doing something you probably wouldn't do—taking a chance." I define risk taking as an opportunity that puts one in a place of discomfort, which in turn creates moments of high

Common Moments When Writers Get Stuck

- Coming up with ideas or when given a prompt
- Revising a writing piece more than once (or at all)
- Trying out a new structure for a whole piece, paragraph, or sentence
- Varying word choice
- Fixing up spelling, punctuation, and capitalization
- Moving from a plan to a first draft
- Sharing writing with others
- Adding voice
- Picturing the audience and writing with that audience in mind
- Writing for a long period of time
- When a formula for the writing is (or is not) given
- When checklists are shared (or not shared) to use for revision and editing
- Beginning, ending, or continuing a writing piece

creativity and engagement. Risk taking requires us to stretch beyond what we are used to—to try something new, often something we have never tried before. To take a risk, one must be vulnerable, and the outcomes can be remarkable! ♟ Here are a few comments about risk taking from students I have met:

Evan: You know that moment [his eyes light up, palm to his chest] when you create something amazing! You know you've taken a risk and it has paid off.

Marek: The pencil keeps moving when you take risks. The ideas come when you push yourself.

Ventia: To take a learning risk is difficult and I get nervous. I think that is because it is hard to pass through it. Even though it is difficult, I think it is worth it!!

Selah: I try to encourage people by telling them there is a big world out there and there are lots of risks you have to take. It is good to believe in yourself.

Aidan: The parts of my writing that I took some risks in were the parts that my classmates liked the best. Those were the parts I got the most feedback on—and they didn't even know that those were risks for me.

These words from writers, willing to try something they have never tried before, show us that taking risks can develop a writer's identity and result in some powerful writing moments.

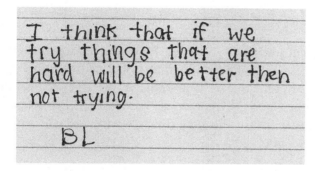

One student's acknowledgment of the growth that can come from risk taking

Risks can pay off, though sometimes it does not seem that way. Felicia, a fourth grader, shared with me a risk she took that did not work out as planned. She wrote a piece on pit bull terriers—a "misunderstood breed," as she called them—and shared it with her next-door neighbor (who was not a pit bull lover). "The neighbor would not even listen," she explained to me, her voice quiet. I didn't say anything; I wanted to have it come from Felicia, how she was handling taking a risk only to be shut down. I didn't rush to "save" her by telling her what she should do next. Instead, I waited.

Felicia added: "I need to write something that will make her listen."

I smiled. "It sounds like you are onto something here—you are not willing to give up trying to make yourself heard," I said, deliberately naming what Felicia was exhibiting in terms of perseverance.

Felicia nodded. "My piece had good facts about pit bulls, but I guess it wasn't good—well, it was good but maybe not persuasive enough."

I tried to paraphrase what she was expressing, in order to support a new risk, when the first didn't work out as planned. "Sounds to me like you want to write an opinion piece that doesn't just share facts, but thinks more carefully about your audience in order to keep them engaged and willing to keep reading. Did I get it right?"

Felicia nodded, ready to take this issue on one more time, ready to revise with that neighbor in mind. I shared a pointer on how she might start (think of what that neighbor values and show how what you are saying fits with her values) and made a plan to follow up at a later time.

In this brief exchange, I helped Felicia recognize a tough reality without being engulfed by it: that just because she writes something does not mean everyone wants to read it. I used her determination to persevere to steer her to setting a specific goal—to write in a way that those who may disagree with her will still want to read her writing.

I could share dozens of similar accounts, of meeting with young writers who are reeling from feeling rebuffed by the world even when they put their best efforts out there. As teachers, it's so important as you and your students embrace the concept of risk taking to convey that these leaps of faith may not always result in the learning we imagine, though it almost always results in learning something, if we let it. Felicia may have just thought, "I am a terrible writer. Nobody is interested in my writing. Why bother?" But she didn't. She made use of her underwater mindframes: persistence and hard work as she navigated disappointment. Hallmarks of a growth mindset.

Let's be real: Risk taking is especially difficult! Writers, who are already working through underwater skills, are also paired with the

The Sorts of Risks Writers Take

If the writer . . .	A risk might be . . .
Spends so much time collecting ideas because she wants the very best one	To just write and not edit her thinking
Always goes with the first idea off the top of his head	To invest more time in collecting more ideas
Hesitates to write a single sentence	To write a number of sentences from which to choose
Writes too much, including unrelated or irrelevant content	To slow down and consider whether what she is writing fits
Feels scared to write	To muster the courage to write anyway
Is concerned about what others think and hesitates to share with others	To share with one trusted classmate, and then another

realization of the social pressures around them. This means that writing (or doing anything new or creative) requires them to try, despite knowing others will see—and judge—their attempts, especially when those attempts end in "failure." I put failure in quote marks because I am not thinking of failure as in getting a failing grade. What I am saying is that writing is all about the moments where we try things out and they simply don't work as we imagined. Risk taking can always have the outcome of failure. This is the reality of risk taking. We may try an idea, a technique of elaboration, a new revision strategy, and despite trying, these fail to work out in our writing. This comfort with embracing failure, and therefore risk taking, is missing in the education world. "The thing I began to notice was not the fear of an 'F,' it was the fear of any mistake," one teacher said. "It's not that students could not get to a final draft, they couldn't get even their ideas down. From a teacher's point of view, that's a nightmare! If students can't take a risk, then certainly they aren't raising their hand with an I-wanna-try-this-idea-out kind of thing" (Lahey, 2015).

And still we know that "innovation requires failure" (Manson, 2013). And the belief that writers must be right on the first try, or that making mistakes or revising ideas is a sign of failure, can stand in the way of true innovation in writing. Therefore, writers must, as Tonya Singer (2014) calls it, "take imperfect action."

Malcolm Gladwell, in his book *Outliers*, shares stories of very successful people. Remarkably, significant proportions of these high achievers are dyslexic or did not complete high school. He attributes their success to being accustomed to failure, for whatever reason, early on in life. They grew comfortable with failure and therefore were more likely to take risks.

Risk Taking: Three Teaching Principles to Live By

In those moments when students are stuck, we need to ignore the instincts that move us to protect our students from risk taking, vulnerability, and failure, and create safe opportunities to try, fail, and try again without shame *in order to learn.*

Brené Brown shares precepts for feedback, and the role we must take on in our conversations with students so that we can sit side by side with them, open and vulnerable, with tender words and a trusting hand. Three of them are particularly useful to support risk taking:

- I can model the vulnerability and openness that I expect to see from you
- I recognize your strengths and how you can use them to address your challenges
- I can talk about how resolving these challenges will lead to your growth and opportunity

I encourage all of us to keep these three principles present (or even her full list of 10 principles, http://brenebrown.com/wp-content/uploads/2013/09/DaringGreatly-EngagedFeedback-8x10.pdf). Print out the list, paste it by your clock, put it in your notebook, make it your computer wallpaper, or print it with your conferring tools, for when we approach our students, open to all they are and all they have put forth, we can begin the essential work of truly celebrating risk taking.

With Brené's precepts in mind, we are ready to give supportive feedback to our writers. Let's get really practical and explore a number of challenges our students face when they feel stuck and consider feedback with an eye toward risk taking.

> I think this means you will never accomplish what you dream, if you don't take the small risk to try.

One writer's reflection

When Writers Feel Stuck Coming Up With Ideas: Strategies to Try

When I asked Maria, a fifth grader, what advice she would give to teachers about writing, she answered, "Let kids have a little freedom to choose what to write about. Let them use their creative mind to dig deeper and think harder. Having freedom to come up with your own ideas makes kids feel like the boss of their own writing." I love that wording, because when kids are bosses of their own writing they have achieved what we want for them: ownership and agency. But to achieve that, we have to let students call the shots—and come up with their own ideas. That means if we feel pressure to use ready-made prompts, we have to resist it. No more of these old chestnuts:

- Write a story about what you did on your summer vacation.
- Write a persuasive piece on whether or not we should wear school uniforms.
- Write a five-paragraph essay on the Boston Massacre.
- Write a Halloween (or turkey) story.
- Write a biography of Neil Armstrong.

Prompts may seem like realistic test prep or efficient, but they completely undermine the self-initiating, creative aspect of writing, and we wind up with a roomful of kids stuck because they "have no ideas." A steady diet of writing to prompts causes students to think that

- Writing is not about or for me. It always starts with someone else's idea.

- We do not write until someone has told us what to write about.

- If I cannot write about that topic, I must be a terrible writer.

- The teacher gave me the prompt, so she must have something in mind for the writing. To do well I must read her mind.

- Writing is only to complete an assignment.

Am I telling you to give the students choice across the board? Absolutely not. As teachers, we can choose the text type (narrative, opinion/argument, informational) and the genre or mode (realistic fiction, book review, feature article). We can also choose broader topics (the American Revolution) in which students can choose their own point of view (women's role in the Revolutionary War, propaganda and the Boston Massacre, Southern slaves siding with Britain to gain freedom). Simply put, we are asking students to make a choice as to what idea they will begin writing from so that they own that idea.

So how do we teach students to generate ideas? 🏰 What I have discovered over the years is the best stories are born from plenty of thinking, rehearsing, and risk taking. The strongest pieces of opinion were mulled over again and again, revising ideas and pinpointing the most persuasive wording. Informational text is richer, more informative, when it does not take on a run-of-the-mill topic but a point of view many may not have considered before. Narratives are more original and well developed when a writer conceptualized the story from the start. Let's explore some ways we can provide opportunities to do this germinating.

Model Strategies for Coming Up With Ideas

Writer's block is alive and well in young writers, just as it is in many adult authors. Coming up with ideas, and sharing those ideas with others, requires a measure of risk taking. Feeling stuck, and not giving up, persevering through the discomfort, and then sharing some preliminary ideas can be very uncomfortable. I am still uncomfortable with this part of the process! There is always the possibility that those ideas will be critiqued and judged, and when that happens I personally feel critiqued and judged. Students can feel the same way. A little lifeline of support helps me take the risk to dig deep, come up with ideas, and share them anyway. That lifeline can come in the form of a strategy.

Strategies are tools we can offer students that help use or access a skill. For instance, if the skill is coming up with ideas, the strategy is one technique or approach to doing this. If the skill is "what" writers need to be able to do, the strategy is "how" to do that. For example, if the skill is to come up with ideas for writing fiction, the strategy may be to think of a story from your own life and consider how it could have gone differently. 🏫

One of the most important things that helps me take a leap to try something new is when I see someone else do it first. I can picture what it looks like, hear what it sounds like, and even get some advice on how to work through trouble. To support our students with risk taking in writing, we can model our own risk-taking strategies by sharing the messy, risky work of taking imperfect action. We share what this feels like, how we work through discomfort to push ourselves further, and the outcomes of this risk. In Brené Brown's words, teachers can "model the vulnerability and openness that I expect to see from you."

Your strategy modeling may start with a notebook of your own. On the facing page is an example from Pam Koutrakos, a third-grade teacher. Notice how she used her notebook to show how she played with ideas and worked them through to write a piece of fiction with "possible ways the story can go." One of the best parts about this is she will have it for all fiction writing instruction for years to come.

This is one small sample of how she has filled her notebook with her own ideas and risks. Pam believes that one of the best ways to support risk taking in writing is to take writing risks herself. I agree. There is simply no alternative to experiencing the hard parts, working through the hard parts, and knowing the sweet excitement when ideas start to take shape—and then using that experience to teach. This approach inspires ideas in the strongest writers—they feel a kinship with their teacher. It inspires ideas in the most challenged writers—they see writing isn't magic, though it can feel magical at points. If we become as vulnerable and open as we expect our students to be, and use our experiences, and our own writing, to show the power of risk taking, the outcome is powerful for the writer and her writing.

I am going to do the same and share my generating-ideas process with you as another example. So here goes (*eek!*): my first collection of ideas for this book, which you can find on page 110.

My ideas are a messy, nonlinear, random collection of possible bits that led to the book itself. Some of what is there made it into this book; much didn't. With all of the work that followed, I consider this the birthplace of the ideas behind this book. To develop and nurture these ideas, long before adding any structure, I met with friends to share and then revised my ideas with their input. What was most important about this phase for me was the space to think freely and

Tip: Create a space for students to generate and work with ideas. Many classrooms use a special notebook, a section of a notebook, or a device. These spaces should feel friendly for taking risks.

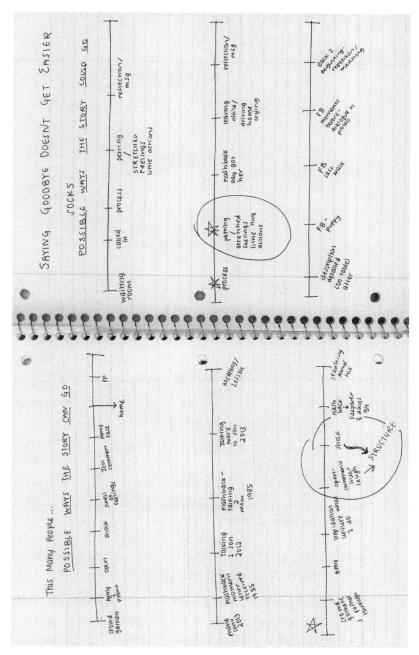

Teacher Pam Koutrakos shares her risk taking as a writer with her students, and in turn, they are more willing to risk take with her.

The seeds of this book. Teach students that initial ideas are supposed to be messy, incomplete, untamed.

work toward an idea of my own, and to be able to reach out when I needed feedback. Students need this as well.

While generating ideas and working on those ideas is crucial to the rest of the writing process, it is also different from writer to writer and piece to piece (as you can see between Pam and me). Some writers sketch, some writers don't use notebooks, others create organizing tools for themselves. Generating ideas and working with those ideas is not exclusive to young writers and their teachers—it spans all ages and experience levels. Check out J. K. Rowling's generating and collecting tool on the next page. No wonder her style for coming up with ideas led to such layered, rich stories!

J. K. Rowling's chapter-by-chapter notes for *The Order of the Phoenix* teach us and our students so many things about the writing process! Whenever I share them with students, they are captivated by them, especially those who are Harry Potter fans. What I like to point out are their very basic aspects: that they are handwritten, as opposed to typed by computer. You might ask: What advantages are there for a writer to write by hand while planning? What do you notice? I notice that in the columns, Rowling is attempting to plan out the flow of time along with the unfolding of the plot, and she is attending to theme. Look at all the crossed-out words, which opens up students to the fact that "messiness" is a natural part of decision making, and that writing is made up of dozens of decisions on the part of the writer. Similarly, the circles, arrows, and parentheses are more evidence that the writer is constantly doing things both to record and ensure that she'll remember her thought processes about these plot points later on. If you have students who have read *The Order of the Phoenix*, challenge them to compare these notes to the published novel.

So let's make this practical for the classroom by pulling the concepts of supporting risk taking by offering strategies and teacher modeling into a practical tool—one that encourages risk taking, supports student ownership, and offers strategies that can be modeled—all to help students come up with ideas. I imagined words students might say when feeling stuck and paired them with possible responses and strategies. My hope is that this tool (see page 113) becomes a way of offering suggestions for trying something new so that risk taking feels supported for your students. I also imagine that you'll add to it with the wording and strategies you find most useful.

When Writers Feel Stuck Elaborating: Strategies to Try

Sometimes writers come up with ideas and run with them only to find themselves stuck on the details of their writing, especially

While we may not be able to decipher every word in Rowling's notes, we can be inspired by the revision of thought, the playful approach, and the complex thinking that was the birth of one of the greatest works of our time. Students can mimic this playfulness in their notebooks.

Language That Supports Risk Taking With Idea Generation

When the kids say . . . 🎯	A response can be . . . ♥	And the strategy might be . . . 🏆
"I'm thinking . . ."	"Yes, thinking is an essential part of writing. We don't want to lose those thoughts as new ones emerge. Let's . . ."	"Think out loud together or with your partner and jot as you go." "Try sketching what you are thinking. Let me show you what I mean."
"I'm stuck. I don't know what to write . . ."	"We have all been at that stuck part. It is important that writers are honest with themselves and share their struggles so that others might support them." "Remember, it's not the story/topic we choose to write about. It is how we write about it."	"Check out our resources [charts, our notebooks, past stories, other authors, etc.]." "Let's set a personal goal for you. I can help." "Let's consider where you are in taking risks [risk-taking learning progression on page 121]."
"I can't come up with any ideas for stories . . . "	"I know that feeling! I can give you some suggestions for what I do when I am stuck." "Because you are thinking so hard about the ideas for your story, you are ready to talk those ideas through with a partner, or me!"	"I think of a person/place and one moment with that person/place." "I think of the firsts or lasts in my life and write a story about one of them." "I imagine a strong emotion and write a story of when I felt that way." "I look to other authors (published or in the classroom) and let their stories inspire my stories."
"I can't come up with any ideas for informational writing . . . "	"I know that feeling! I can give you some suggestions for what I do when I am stuck." "Because you are feeling stuck, you are ready to try a different strategy."	"I think of a topic I know a whole lot about and would like to teach others about." "I think of something I do on my free time and think, 'What can I teach others about this topic?'" "I look to other authors (published or in the classroom) and let their topics inspire my topics."
"I can't come up with any ideas for opinion/ argument writing . . ."	"I know that feeling! I can give you some suggestions for what I do when I am stuck." "Because you have very careful tastes about the ideas you are writing down, you are ready to rehearse."	"I think of those things that really bug me." "I think of what I want to change and who can help me change it." "I think of a problem and what I can do to solve it."

Available for download at **http://resources.corwin.com/McGee-Feedback**

the sorts of details that move their writing forward. Undoubtedly, many writers often have moments where they are struck by inspiration, but once they put the pencil to paper they freeze. Maybe you have writers who are strong at talking about an idea but once they are met with a blank sheet of paper, they shut down. While there may be many reasons for these sorts of stuck moments, perhaps these writers are intimidated and stumped by adding some details to those grand, inspired writing ideas. Maybe they are not sure what details to add, or maybe they are following a strict structure that feels too constraining. Maybe they are overwhelmed by the amount of details they have already come up with and simply do not know where to start. They may need some feedback to help them nudge themselves out of this sort of logjam. 👓 Where to start?

Find and name the treasures in the writing.

The first stop is to start with what *is* working. 🎯 ⚓ Though sometimes it can feel counterintuitive, naming what the writer has done that is strong can help them push through the hard parts and elaborate. In Katherine Bomer's book *Hidden Gems: Naming and Teaching From the Brilliance in Every Student's Writing* (2010), we learn the power of being able to mine student writing for strengths, celebrating those strengths, and empowering students to work from those strengths to continue growing. These are beautiful and powerful teaching moves.

As Katherine acknowledged, the "mistakes" in writing tend to jump out at us and very often our students. I think this is what we have been conditioned to do—look for errors and help correct those errors. This, after all, is how most of us learned writing. To be clear, these "mistakes" aren't something to ignore, just something to put in second place to the strengths that exist in the writing.

By naming strengths, we first acknowledge the work that has been done thus far, because often writers may be unaware of those strengths. It is important to trust that there is always, always something to consider a strength.

We begin by naming what is working and follow up next steps. ⚓ Let's try it out by revisiting Zack's piece from Chapter 3:

> # Harry Potter
> ## Book Review
> Rating: ✮✮✮✮✮ *Five stars!*
>
> JK Rowling is a pionner. She made the first, as I like to call it, "special Kid" series. Basicly, she made the idea of a regular Kid having super awesome powers. The daringness of pioneering a genre, for goodness sake, is just amazing. Second, the realness of the whole book ties right in with our world. The wizard takes in "muggle" things is quirky and comical. Also, this book series has way more plot twists than a usual book, but just enough to make it unique.
>
> These are just a few things the series blends into its mix. But even how good a book is that has "move over, Harry Potter" on the back, I say, Harry "aint goin' nowhere"!

Some strengths I noticed:

1. **Voice:** I can hear this author's personality coming through in phrases like "for goodness sake" and "Harry ain't goin' nowhere."
2. **Organization:** This author introduced the book a bit, said something about it, and then wrapped it up.
3. **Comma usage:** This author used commas often to add pauses, which created a passionate tone.

Name the next steps as "readiness". 🎯 🏆

There is some very simple, and powerful, language that I found works with writers taking risks.

Because you . . . you are ready for . . . ♥

Because you structured your piece so carefully, you are ready to elaborate.

Because you were so careful with your word choice, you are ready to play around with some more examples from the book.

> Because you bring in your voice so clearly, you are ready to quote the text.

This wording shows strengths and next steps.  It shows that we are looking out for strengths in order to highlight them and celebrate them. It sets us up to use one of the essentials of feedback from Brené Brown: using strengths to tackle challenges. It also sends the message that there have been successes and those successes have put you in a place of accomplishment—the next steps wouldn't be possible otherwise.

© Rick Harrington Photography

Let's explore a few ways that this wording can work to support writers with the trickiest parts of elaborating.

Model the elaboration.

Just as we model risk taking in coming up with ideas, we might also model elaborating. Sometimes we sit with students and mentor text in hand as a way to show a variety of elaboration techniques. We might open up a purposefully chosen book to point out the elaboration craft that the author used. We might then ask our students to try out that craft as well. But sometimes, this is not enough, and even the most wonderful mentor text can't help our writers become unstuck by simply looking at the writing. Here is when we can bring in modeling and even use some bare bones writing to model.

Language That Supports a Writer's Risk Taking During Revision

What You Might Notice 🎯	Wording You Might Use 🏆
If the writer is stuck coming up with ways to revise stories . . .	"Because you have worked so hard at getting ideas down, you are ready to talk those ideas through with a partner, or me!" "Because you have such strong organization, with a beginning, middle, and end, you are ready to add some story elements. You might want to try dialogue, talking, or thinking." "Because you have been so detailed in your use of dialogue, you are ready to weave in some action and description."
If the writer is stuck coming up with ways to revise informational text . . .	"Because you were able to get the table of contents written for your information book, you are ready to try out different ways of structuring your chapters." "Because you have such clear chapters and information in those chapters, you are ready to add some graphics to support your information." "Because your information is so clear, you are ready to include some domain-specific words (or transitional language, etc.)."
If the writer is stuck coming up with ways to revise opinion/argument pieces . . .	"Because you have stated your claim clearly, you are ready to plan out your most convincing reasons." "Because you included many reasons in your favor, you are ready to try to address the counterargument." "Because you have clearly included many factual supports for your claim, you are ready to bring in a few anecdotes."

 Available for download at **http://resources.corwin.com/McGee-Feedback**

Bare bones writing is a piece of teacher-written text that is intentionally missing a particular elaboration technique (this term is used often in my professional circle, but I cannot seem to find the origin of it!). It is usually written with the student's current writing in mind. In other words, if the writing is missing dialogue, we write a piece intentionally leaving dialogue out. 🎯 If the writing is missing direct citations, we leave those out. The teacher then models the thinking process and writing steps she or he takes when using that needed technique, adding it directly into the writing and talking it through when doing so. ♥ On the facing page is an example of the before and after of bare bones writing. Notice how I started with a piece of narrative writing that was written without adding thoughts or feelings. I modeled in front of the student(s) how I add thoughts and feelings to elaborate, talking through my process of choosing where, why, and how I added these details. Basically, I talked through each step as I elaborated, sounding like a how-to. ♥

Let's take a moment to revisit the steps of the process to help students elaborate when they are stuck. What I love most about this process is that it avoids the correcting lens and instead supports students to try something that stretches them and their writing, grounded in a place of strength and ownership. It boils down to three steps: 🏛

1. Name the treasures

2. Call the next steps "readiness"

3. Model the technique

Steps for Using Bare Bones Writing

1. Notice a challenge a student is having in her writing.

2. Write a short piece that includes that same challenge.

3. Model for the writer how to improve on that challenge.

Tip 1: Keep your bare bones writing in a page protector and model using a dry erase marker so you can wipe it off and model with it again in the future.

Tip 2: Keep in mind that bare bones writing will not sound complete or even close to fully elaborated when modeling with it—in fact, it shouldn't. It is there to model a writing technique or strategy, not be an exemplar of the genre. Writing a quick, unelaborated piece is all that is needed, so don't feel the pressure to write it with great care. This will save you time.

Welcome Nessa

The car pulled up and
turned into our driveway.
My husband tooted the
horn to announce their
arrival. I ran over
to the car, seeing Shannon
through the window smiling.
One I opened the car
door, I could see the
reason for Shannon's smile.
She held Nessa, our new puppy,
gently in her arms.

Bare bones writing before demo without the elaboration strategy of adding thoughts and feelings

---

Welcome Nessa

The car pulled up and *while my heart beat loudly in anticipation.*^
turned into our driveway. ^
My husband tooted the
horn to announce their *"What have I gotten myself into?" I thought.*
arrival. ^ I ran over
to the car, seeing Shannon *a wave of relief and joy washed over me.*^
through the window smiling. ^
I tried to picture this new little one in my mind.^
One I opened the car
door, I could see the
reason for Shannon's smile.
Pears pricked my eyes as I gazed down at this white bundle.^
She held Nessa, our new puppy,
gently in her arms.

Bare bones writing after demo with thoughts and feelings added

119

When Writers Feel Stuck With Taking Risks: Strategies to Try

When taking risks, sometimes we need a little inspiration. This graphic inspires me when I need to push myself to take risks, and it reassures me during moments I want to retreat into a place of safety. When I have been in places of discomfort in writing, in my work, in moments of creativity, I find that I have also learned, significantly—it is where the magic happens. This graphic reminds me to live out of my comfort zone sometimes.

A learning progression is a tool that students and teachers can use to mark and work toward a particular level of mastery. For more information on learning progressions and how they are used go to http://edglossary.org/learning-progression.

As much as we hope our students can take the support we have given them and run with it, it is more than likely that risk taking is not the most comfortable concept and may be a touchy place to receive feedback. One of my favorite tools for giving feedback and supporting students' agency is a learning progression. Learning progressions are very popular, yet they need to be carefully used to support student independence and choice making. When used well, learning progressions can develop agency and ownership through self-assessment and next steps. Check out the following learning progression:

Risk Taking in My Learning Journey

Safe and Sound	A Bit on the Edge	Pushing Myself	Out of My Comfort Zone
I went with the first idea off the top of my head. I am done in a snap. I am bored.	I didn't stop right away. I came up with a few more ideas. I am asking friends and teachers for approval of my ideas.	I am writing all of the ideas in my mind and then digging deeper to find even more. When I share with others I am asking specific questions about my ideas and what I have tried. I feel excited about what I have come up with.	I am coming up with even more ideas and it feels like hard work. I am pushing past the feelings of discomfort and continuing to find the ideas that are important to me. I am pleasantly surprised by the ideas that I come up with.

When using a learning progression, students may find it useful as a planning and reflection tool. It is also an extremely helpful tool in supporting the underwater mindframes of hard work and persistence. We want to be sure to show students how to use it to its fullest potential. It is not meant to be a moment of teacher diagnosis.

How **NOT** to Use the Learning Progression	How to Use the Learning Progression
Sit down with the student, browse through their notebook, and tell them that they are probably in the "bit on the edge" column and need to go to the "pushing myself column."	Sit down with the student and introduce the learning progression by sharing what it is and why we use it. Share what will happen to their writing if they reach toward column 3 or 4. Share where you might be and what you will do to plan for the next steps. Then coach the student to do the same. This can be done in a whole group as well.

The many purposes of this learning progression:

1. To support student ownership over their process.
2. To share a vision of where to go and create next steps.
3. To give specifics on writing habits, not just skills.
4. To create more independent writers who make choices.
5. To support partnership conversations on risk taking.
6. To provide teachers with the language we can use to support risk taking.

Please know that learning progressions are most useful when they are tailored for the students you work with and are not meant to be a grading tool. ◎ If you revise this tool for your class, it will be even more useful! Lesa Jezequel from Dater School in Ramsey, New Jersey, created a staple in her classroom with this concept, yet added her own wording and imagery (see the next page).

A learning progression isn't one-size-fits-all, but instead is customized for different learners on different trajectories. Different students in your class may have different learning progressions based on the type of writer or type of risk they may need to take (see types of risk chart on page 103). So use these examples to inspire your own!

Some student reactions—both sweet and enlightening—to using this learning progression:

Jake: Getting to where the magic happens has been going well. I've worked to try things I never had before.

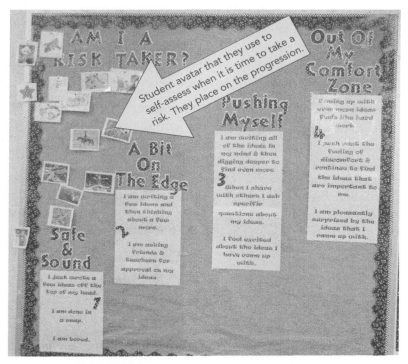

Lesa made public risk taking by creating this interactive bulletin board, implying that risk taking is something we all must do as writers.

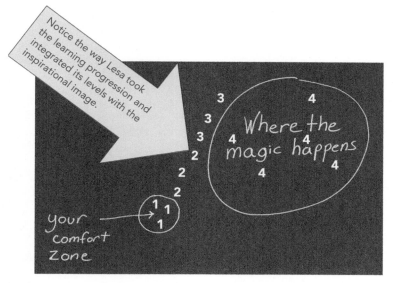

Student writers really "get" this classroom display. Never underestimate the power of charts to convey high expectations in an appealing manner.

Tara: Using this helps me work harder to get to the level I want to be at. I know I have moved when I feel good about my ideas. I feel good after I have dug deeper. Also, one of the things up there is talking to other people and them telling you advice on how to improve your story. This helped me.

Felicia: I took risks because of this board. It was hard and I tried. I learned that not all of my writing risks or ideas work out but my writing got stronger.

All in all, we are looking to create a trusting, celebratory environment where risk taking, especially when mistakes or failure are the result, is encouraged, supported, and celebrated. When risk taking at the right moments is part of a writer's work, growth is inevitable.

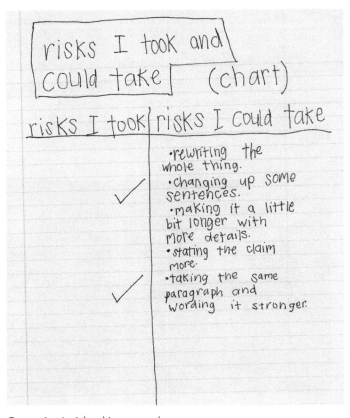

One writer's risk-taking record

Techy Risk Taking

Technology has created opportunities for virtual feedback given over a device in the form of comments. How can we still support the concept of risk taking when we are not face to face and avoid the misinterpretation of written comments? Here are some pointers:

1. Start from strengths. When giving comments, use the phrasing "because you . . . you are ready for . . ."

2. Use the wording from the tools in this chapter to set the tone. Many times comments can be misread, so carefully chosen wording is key. Check back to Chapters 1 and 3 for more information on this sort of wording as well.

3. Note when you believe a student has taken a risk and celebrate that vulnerability.

4. If you need to say something that is hard to word and may be sensitive to hear, try to do that face to face. Remember, these comments can be read by parents as well.

5. While it may be easy to comment on everything, choose feedback on just those three or four significant items that can be used throughout the writing. Commenting on a single piece of missing punctuation is not as helpful as suggesting an elaboration technique that can be used often in the piece.

4. See Chapter 5 on designing written feedback for more pointers.

Wrapping It Up

Inviting students to become risk takers nurtures them to become better problem solvers, to grow more creative, and to engage as critical thinkers. Through comfort, choice, and having a safe zone for taking risks, students become better prepared for the future that awaits them. From the power of risk taking, we explore other, impactful, important, and nontraditional ways of supporting students' writing and writing identity. 👓 Next stop, feedback when it is time to stretch and grow, with a focus on goal setting.

Chapter 5

When It Is Time to Stretch and Grow
Feedback for Goal Setting

What you get by achieving your goals is not as important as what you become by achieving your goals.

—Henry David Thoreau

Kate DiCamillo is one of the most revered authors publishing today, yet she came into writing "late" in her life. She was an English major, knew she had a talent to write, and writing stories was always one of her dreams. But it was not until 1994, when she was about 30 years old, that she realized that she needed to do more than believe in her talent; she needed to act upon it. She'd hit a point in her life where she knew it was time to kick it up a notch. She set herself a goal. She made a commitment to write two pages a day, 5 days a week. Within a year, the first draft of *Because of Winn Dixie* was finished (still my favorite book of hers!) and her life as a professional author began. It has been over 20 years of writing two pages a day, and because of this goal, she has written some of the most beloved and award-winning books of our time.

Writers of all ages can learn from Kate DiCamillo's experience and choices. When writers find themselves at a crossroads of complacency or disengagement, or when it is simply time to kick it up a notch and do something bigger and better in writing, setting goals pushes a writer to stretch and grow. In our writing classrooms, we need to look for ways to orient lessons and our coaching around explicit attention to goal setting, and laced throughout this book are ideas for doing just that.

In this chapter, we look at the feedback centered around working toward goals, which can result in outcomes for students never achieved before. Remember Felicia, the student I introduced in Chapter 4 who was arguing that pit bulls are a misunderstood breed? Listen to where goal setting took her as a writer: "My goal is to use my voice to correct misunderstandings by sharing facts. Working with this goal made me realize that I never knew I had such a big voice. I never thought of putting my voice out into the world for change. And with this goal, I now know I can make change through writing."

Goal setting can help us take aim at something beyond our current ability and push us to achieve what we never thought was possible— in all areas of our lives, whenever we want to stretch and grow. And goal setting in the writing classroom is one of the most practical and powerful teaching moves we can make, especially when we support reaching goals with lots and lots of meaningful, effective feedback.

Examples of Student Goals

"My goal is to tell the reader my ideas and opinion of a text and help them understand with reasons." —Rose, Grade 3

"I want to make my reasons support my opinion in a clear and strong way." —Nora, Grade 4

"My goal is to write without getting distracted." —Owen, Grade 4

"I am aiming to write less and include only what is important or relevant to the piece." —Liv, Grade 6

"Write a counterargument without changing my stance in the rest of the piece." —Jackson, Grade 7

"Write using a variety of sentence structures with accurate and more sophisticated punctuation." —Brien, Grade 8

Goal Setting: A Few Essentials

People who set goals and work to reach those goals are more successful—in life, in work, in school. Working toward a goal is motivating, which therefore yields stronger results (Locke, 1968). Goals refine our focus, putting energies into just a few outcomes, channeling our work and sharpening its influence. Goal setting can, therefore, move writers forward, as long as there are a few important characteristics of those goals. Hattie (2012) found that "there is strong evidence that challenging, achievable goals influence achievement, *provided the individual is involved in setting them.*" Locke and Latham (2006) state that "achievement is enhanced to the degree that teachers set challenging, rather than 'do your best' goals, relative to the students' present competencies. There is a direct linear relationship between the degree of goal difficulty and performance."

So what's the practical, classroom takeaway from this research? We have to do this work *with* the students, and not *for* the students. As we set goals, we also have to consider the level of difficulty, so that students design goals that are not too difficult, ending in frustration, not too easy, where no learning happens, but just right. As Hattie puts it, "goals have a self-energizing effect if they are appropriately challenging as they can motivate students to exert effort in line with the difficulty or demands of the goal" (2011, p. 164).

  ## PBs: Personal Bests

One concept that is being successfully used in many classrooms, described by A. J. Martin, professor of educational psychology at the University of New South Wales (2014), suggests that we support students in setting goals that are considered personal bests (PBs). He defines PBs as "specific, challenging, competitively self-referenced targets toward which individuals strive." Martin also found that, though born in the athletic world, "personal bests had high positive relationships to educational aspirations, enjoyment of school, participation in class and persistence on the task." Just what we hope for from each writer. Goal setting for personal bests is hardly arguable, but it is a bit of an art.

> I think writing with a goal in mind is good so you can write great ideas, and still get to do that one thing that will really just top it all off.

Students do better with goal setting when they have opportunities to define its benefits in their own words.

To begin, we can support writers to think either about writer-centered or writing-centered goals. 👓 Kate DiCamillo thought of a writer-centered goal—to commit to putting in the day-to-day hours and effort it takes to write. Felicia had a writing-centered goal—to use her writing to make change in the world. Here are other examples of writing versus writer-centered goals (more on a step-by-step process for setting goals in the next section):

Writer-Centered Goals: Personal goals for the writer	Writing-Centered Goals: A larger purpose for the writing, or specific writing techniques to use
Make the most of writing time by writing more each day.	Convince the principal to have library time for middle schoolers.
Meet with partners and ask specific questions.	Tell a story that shows one solution for bullying in school.
Use feedback to make revisions.	Structure writing to be most convincing.
Commit to trying something new in writing even if I feel nervous.	Use different sentence structures, including simple, compound, complex, and compound-complex to be clear in explaining information.

Writer-Centered Goals: Personal goals for the writer	Writing-Centered Goals: A larger purpose for the writing, or specific writing techniques to use
Center back on my writing when my mind wanders.	Use flashback and symbolism to convey the theme of the story.
Embrace disappointment and mistakes as opportunities to learn something new.	Create clarity and coherence through specific word choice.
Persevere when writing is hard for me.	Write with the audience of my peers in mind and choose specific supports that will appeal to them.

Goals can be set at different points in the year and in the writing process. Here are a few ideas on when you may support goal setting:

- **Kicking off the year:** Thinking ahead to what the school year can hold, there is a hopefulness of possibilities that makes it a prime time to set goals.

- **Kicking off a unit:** At the onset of a unit of study, focused on a particular text type, students can design goals that will be a focus throughout the unit. These goals can help us give very specific feedback.

- **Kicking off a writing piece:** When students are writing something in a short amount of time, about an hour or less, they can quickly set goals and keep them in mind as they write so the final product is as strong as it can be.

- **Kicking off each day:** What are the little goals that will help writers meet the big goals? Thinking about them every day can result in stronger writers and writing.

I think it is important to keep a goal in my mind because then I know what I am aiming for. Also then I would know what I want to complete at the end of the unit.

Ask students to reflect on the purpose and power of goal setting as part of instruction on what makes a goal strong.

How to Set and Use Goals Effectively

Yes, there is an art to setting goals. The first step is defining, for ourselves and our students, what makes a strong goal. There are many schools of thought out there, but I think the simplest approach is to consider three big concepts/ingredients to design useful goals. Let's take a moment, then, to identify the three Cs of a strong, useful goal: Clarity, Challenge, and Commitment (Locke & Latham, 2006).

- **Clarity:** Strong goals are specific and clear. Writers know what their goals mean and can begin to articulate how to reach them. Keep in mind that clear goals can be set around both the writer and the writing. Writer-centered goals may be more about how the writer within would like to stretch and grow: Identify my strengths and use them intentionally, bring my voice into my writing, capture the spirit of my relationship with my grandmother in my personal narrative. Writing-centered goals may be more about the process and product: Use a variety of sentence structures, elaborate using narrative details, ensure pronoun agreement. Whatever the goal, it should be specific and clear.

Examples of Clear Goals	Examples of Vague Goals
Use the story elements to write realistic fiction.	Write a realistic fiction story well.
Elaborate using details that teach the readers about the topic such as examples, anecdotes, and content-specific words to add voice and originality to my information writing.	Add details.
Spell words correctly by using all available resources.	Get better at spelling.
Take my time when writing descriptions of my surroundings, adding in sensory details that convey how I felt and how nature changed my perspective.	Help my reader connect with nature by writing more.
Use my love of dialogue to work on scenes between characters that move my story along and show the conflict between the characters.	Get better at writing short stories.

- **Challenge:** ◎ Remember Vygotsky's Zone of Proximal Development (ZPD)—likely something you spent a lot of time studying in undergrad or graduate school? ZPD is very relevant to goal setting. I envision ZPD like an imaginary bubble around a learner's head, almost like an old-fashioned astronaut or deep-sea diver's helmet. Anything within that bubble is attainable, yet ambitious, and not yet learned—it is in the zone of challenge. The writer can see and imagine using that learning, but it has not yet become part of his skill set. Any learning beyond the bubble is simply too far away, too challenging, and should be part of a later goal when the student is ready. The teacher, who is continually observing, listening, and formatively assessing, helps students identify what is within that zone and set a goal at the appropriate level of challenge. This is the Goldilocks level of challenge—not too hard, not too easy, just right. More on how to do this later in the chapter.

- **Commitment:** Writers must commit to a goal, owning it and setting their sights on it. This commitment may come from within, as goals bubble up from a want or a need. The goal may come from the heart, with writers saying, "I see so many of my classmates who are hurt by so-called friends. I want to write a story that can show them how to deal with these sorts of situations." Or it may come from the head: "I am going to write to Jim Arnosky to ask him how he got started because I want to be a writer like him too and I am worried that manatees might become extinct soon." Wherever the goal arises, whether from the heart or head, writers choose the goals themselves, with support as needed, but in the end the choice is truly theirs. With that commitment comes a long-term investment to stick with the goal or even adjust it if necessary. There is great ownership on the part of the writer.

The Many Possibilities to "CCC" Set Goals

To create highly effective goals, there must be great ownership of these goals by the student. "Specifically, when students set their own goals, they take responsibility and ownership of their learning goals. Such goal-directed behavior that results from goal setting is empowering and proactive" (Elliot & Fryer, 2008). There are a

© Rick Harrington Photography

variety of techniques you might use to support young writers in creating goals that they own and therefore toward which they work. Choosing which approach depends on your writers. If they have never chosen a goal for themselves before, you might want to go with a more supportive technique. If they are already somewhat introspective, maybe use a technique that has a little less teacher direction. I am sharing these approaches in loose order from most supported goal-setting approach to least supported goal-setting tools.

Student Ownership in Goal Setting

If your writers have never had the chance to design goals for themselves, you may want to choose a very supportive approach to goal selection. You may also want to use this very supportive approach only for the few students who have difficulty choosing goals if others are able to do so with more independence. What is crucial about this approach is that we do not take too much ownership out of the hands of the writers. After all, commitment, as we know, is one of the three essentials of goal setting, and having choice in goal setting can nurture commitment. Following are a few ways you may consider supporting goal selection while also giving writers ownership of the goals.

Personal Goal Selection From Class Goals

The first approach you might take is to start off your writers with the goals you have already set for the unit or writing experience. I want to underscore that in encouraging students to select their own goals, I don't mean "anything goes." As adults and teachers, we know the grade-level skills and curricula we want them to hit, and the attributes of writing well, so it makes sense that our students draw from this well of possibilities when they consider writing goals. An example of Brianne's unit goals is featured below. Writers can then choose and commit to a goal they believe will help them the most. The wording and design are done for them, but the choice is still theirs. 🏛

Persuasive Writing Unit Goals:	How to Set Student Goals From Unit Goals
❋ writers generate focused ideas for persuasive topics. ❋ writers elaborate using details & text evidence. ❋ writers use grammar and conventions to convey ideas clearly. ❋ writers chose precise details and facts to help make their point and use figurative language to draw readers in their line of thought.	1. Introduce and explain the unit goals. You may want to show examples of each goal in a piece of writing such as a mentor text or student sample. 2. Ask students to choose a goal or two that helps them grow or challenges them in some way. 3. Ask students to write down the goal and explain how reaching that goal will help them grow or list some ideas/steps on how they will meet their goal.

Notice in the unit goals that there are plenty of rigor and skill expectations, but also plenty of room for students to interpret, experiment, and goal set in ways relevant to them and their current work.

Goal Selection From Teacher-Designed Choices

Another approach you may want to take is to create a menu, of sorts, from which students can choose goals, as Pam Koutrakos, a third-grade teacher, did in the sample that follows. One reason why I love Pam's approach is that it is so specific. She lists a quality of writing or writers and then lists details or directions within that quality. In other words, goals are not just about structure, but honing in on one part of structure. I also like the option of the teacher choosing a goal—this allows the teacher to customize student goals to be more or less challenging, depending on the writer. You may notice as you use this approach, as Pam did, that as the school year progresses, the teacher and student goals start to match one another more and more.

How to Set Unit Goals From a List

1. List the qualities of strong writing or writers (e.g., structure, elaboration).
2. Underneath each quality, break down and detail that quality. For example, if you list structure, you may include paragraph, introduction, overall, etc.
3. Describe and explain the parts and pieces of this tool so that your writers understand, at least loosely, what they mean.
4. Ask students to select a focus.
5. Choose a focus as well.
6. Ask students to write down the goal and explain how reaching that goal will help them grow, or ask them to list some ideas/steps on how they will meet their goal.

Polishing and Articulating Goals for the Writer

Another option is to talk with the writer and help him come up with a goal that perhaps he could not have designed by himself.

Student: Month(s)/Unit: *Opinion Writing*

WRITING GOAL SHEET

☐ Work on structure

- o   Inclusion of ingredients
- o   Opening/Beginning
- o   Body/Middle
- o   Closing/End
- ☒   Transitions   STUDENT GOAL

☐ Work on elaboration

- o   Stretching heart
- o   Including inside & outside thoughts
- o   Different scenes/settings
- ☒   Details, examples, evidence - TEACHER GOAL

☐ Work on process

- o   Initiation
- o   Effort
- o   Stamina
- o   Independence in moving through the writing process

☐ Work on craft/voice

- o   Leads
- o   Thesis
- o   Figurative Language
- o   Theme
- o   Persuasive Language

☐ Work on meaning/significance

- o   Considering audience when choosing which details to include

☐ Work on conventions/mechanics

NOTES:

Students keep writing goal sheets in their notebooks, and to keep them vital, I recommend they look back at these goals often, at least every few days, to consider their progress toward their goal(s).

With this type of goal-setting conference, I might sit with a student at the onset of a unit or writing piece. I dig a bit to find out where that writer is in terms of the unit goals or standards, and also where he is in his intentions for his own writing or writerly life. For example, fourth grader Felicia had no idea where to start and did not have a goal imagined in her head, but she was able to talk about herself as a writer. Felicia's goal was designed by talking through her writing identity. We talked first about what matters most to her in her life to focus on her passions and emotions—the place where writing originality, voice, and heart are born. Realizing she was a writer who feels a call to action to correct misunderstandings, we set that as a goal. My role in this conversation was to listen carefully and work on articulating and polishing what Felicia was having difficulty finding words to describe. Felicia later reflected that she had never thought about writing or herself in this way. This approach

	How to Design Goals From Conversation
Use your voice to correct misunderstandings with facts.	1. Talk to the student and ask about her passions, emotions, thoughts, feelings, wishes, wants, worries, etc.
	2. Paraphrase what he is saying and add some of your own thinking to the discussion.
	3. Propose a goal and ask what the student thinks about it.
	4. Jot down the goal, or ask the student to jot down the goal.
	5. Ask the student to jot down the goal and explain how reaching that goal will help her grow. Or list some ideas/steps on how the student will meet his goal.

Steps to get to my writing goals

- I start doing what's necessary
- Then I do what's possible
- And then I'm doing my goals

One student's plan for meeting her goal

Goal

I want to choose expert. words to teach readers a lot about the subject. I want to teach information in a way to intrust readers. I may use drawings, captions or diagrams.

First, I will make sure I add in things like pictures and captions. Next, I will add in detail to make my writing stronger. Then, I will make sure I keep this goal in mind to help me complete my goal. After that, I will add in how-to steps and tips to make my website better. Finally, I will read over my website and add in finishing touches.

Another student's plan for meeting his goal

also works well when a goal does not seem challenging enough and you want to walk through the process so students discover, and own, bigger possibilities. 🐢 🎯

Many students need great support in designing goals, which teachers can provide through feedback, and the above approaches can help them do so with clarity, challenge, and commitment. We can also approach goal setting with a little less support and more student ownership, as highlighted in the following approaches.

Using Student Reflection to Set Goals

When thinking about supporting students and yet not doing the heavy lifting ourselves in goal setting, reflection can be a handy tool. When we offer suggestions for reflection and next steps, students can do more of the thinking work and we can simply facilitate

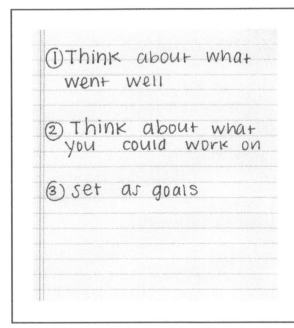

	How to Use Reflection to Set Goals
① Think about what went well ② Think about what you could work on ③ set as goals	1. Share the reflection process, shown in the photograph to the left. 2. Using a piece of your own writing, model this reflection process, naming what went well, what you want to work on, and how you create specific goals from this. 3. Ask students to give it a try, ideally with a writing partner. 4. After students have written down the goal and explained how reaching it will help them grow, or listed some ideas/steps on how they will meet their goal, have students meet in small groups to share their goals and steps, asking for ideas and feedback.

Notice in the unit goals that there are plenty of rigor and skill expectations, but also plenty of room for students to interpret, experiment, and goal set in ways relevant to them and their current work.

that thinking. We are not totally hands-off, but the student is in the driver's seat. Because of this, the reflective approach is my personal favorite. I have designed a simple three-step process that teachers have really loved using and found effective. First, they are often pleasantly surprised to see how much the students already know about themselves and their writing. Second, teachers share that they like starting from strengths, having previously thought of goals as exclusively working on a weakness. In fact, many have shared that the hardest part for writers is to identify personal strengths, yet they are quick to list many challenges. Writers can really be tough on themselves.

Pam also did something similar yet in a more informal way. On the next page is a note she left in one of her students' writer's note-books, suggesting it was time for a little reflection and goal setting to help that writer the next day and for days to come. She personalized the time for goal setting, depending on when the student was ready to take that next step, and she did so through a quick jot on a sticky note. Wise, powerful, guiding words that can easily be replicated. I also admire the tone she takes—she is like a coach giving advice who is also respectful of the writer and the writer's process.

Combining Feedback and Intention to Set Goals

On page 143 is one incredible combination, from fifth-grade teacher Laura Sarsten, using the concepts of feedback, intention, investment, and learning slogans to set goals. I am in awe of the sophistication of this process, its useful outcomes for students, and the inspiration it provides when working to meet goals. I also love the wording Laura uses here. For example, she uses the word *intention* instead of *goal*. While intentions are not exactly goals, they are quite similar. An intention includes a purpose that aligns one's attitude and wishes to achieve something larger in life. In the classroom, intentions and goals can be used synonymously or simultaneously. And, while goals often have next steps, Laura uses the word *investment* instead, which is another larger, more purposeful

> Take some time to honestly reflect on your experience & try to figure out what worked for you... & what didn't.
>
> When you know what works — you can keep doing it... & become more successful.
>
> By figuring out what didn't work for us, we know to also try to avoid that in the future.

Never underestimate the power of a well-timed personal note to a writer. So many students need these impromptu "I see you" messages from us, notes that let them know that when they stall or have setbacks, we aren't judging them but seeing clues for future success.

word that includes not just next steps but also attitudes and dispositions. Finally, the motivating learning slogan, self-chosen by the student, adds that bit of inspiration and cheerleading that helps writers reach further. Laura's process, for this sophisticated experience, is pretty simple, as described in the following chart.

How to Combine Feedback, Intentions, and Learning Slogans to Set Goals

1. Ask students to look back at feedback they received from peers, teachers, and themselves. Review past work and recollect discussions with writing partners.

2. Ask students to talk about how they are going to respond to that feedback. Ask them to consider what actions they might take to interact and use the feedback that was given. Set this as the intention and investment.

3. Last, ask students to look inward toward their own learning attitudes and come up with a personalized slogan to which they felt connected, thinking about where they want to take their learning next and how the motivating slogan would resemble that.

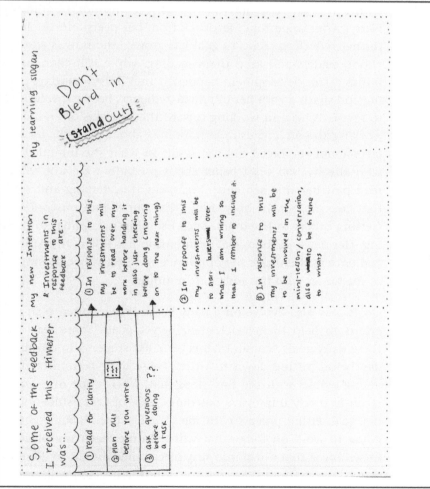

If this chart were posted on Facebook, I'd hit the "Love" button 10 times! Our student writers can develop so much more when we approach writing as something they can control, personalize, and "bend to their will" with a learning slogan.

The Evolution of Goals

The upcoming section is all about ways our young writers can get feedback on their goals—both from teachers and from peers. As we move into that section, there is one important thing to keep in mind: The goals our young writers start with are likely not the goals with which they will end. Along the way, and often as a result of feedback, goals evolve, becoming more tailored, traveling in different directions, being replaced altogether, or giving birth to baby goals (smaller goals that are born from larger goals). Goals should be pliable and responsive as a writer learns more. Felicia, whom I mentioned earlier in this chapter and in previous chapters, started with this goal: "Use my voice to correct misunderstandings with facts." After some time, feedback from her peers and teacher, and further reflection, Felicia's goal has grown. She now is working to "hook readers and keep them reading, while still changing their minds." This development happened after only a few days of drafting and sharing with her intended audience, before she even began to revise. Felicia, in working toward the first version, noticed that working to correct misunderstandings about pit bulls by sharing facts about the breed did not result in what she intended. Those who already had a set belief about pit bulls were not willing to read past her first sentence. We spent time talking and realizing that facts are not the only things that can change misconceptions. Getting others to listen and keep listening is essential to persuading. Her newly revised goal or intention has Felicia thinking about audience as she shares her opinion, and selectively choosing words as she writes with the audience in mind.

Goals may also evolve on a daily basis. Writers often plan smaller efforts to help them reach their bigger goals. Some teachers call these daily goals "commitments" and ask students to do this every day before sitting down to write. These daily commitments help young writers with the tiny steps that, when done over and over, result in pretty impressive outcomes. One of Lesa's students shared her goal-setting process with me: "First, I think about what I am going to work on today that will help me reach my bigger goal. I then break that down into tiny pieces and commit to doing those things. For example, I am not the fastest writer, so I will often push myself to write to a certain number of lines and plan in small breaks for myself." These microgoals or daily commitments are, in fact, a larger goal broken down with even more detail. They also build in the space for other goals to come into play, especially those that are more about habits and new learning.

  ## Feedback on Goals From Classmates

Reaching a goal can go a lot more smoothly, and be a lot more fun, when we turn to others for feedback. We as teachers certainly can give feedback on goals, and we will in so many ways. Let's not forget, though, that we are not the only teachers of writing in our classrooms—all of our students are as well. Tapping into feedback from peer to peer can go a long way in supporting writers in meeting their goals. I'm especially inspired by the words of Anne Davies (2003) when she writes, "Feedback nourishes the learning brain [but] as long as teachers see themselves as the sole source of feedback, students will not receive as much as they need to learn." Yet we may worry a bit, knowing that students don't always make the most of feedback opportunities. Sometimes, when giving feedback, students may sit in awkward silence. Or the opposite—students may talk about everything except the writing. Even worse, in my opinion, is when one writer takes another writer's paper and does the "correcting" for him. Not a lot of learning goes on there!

© Rick Harrington Photography

One way of addressing these potential pitfalls is to set up students with a protocol that can structure and guide the conversation toward strong, meaningful feedback. When giving feedback in the frame of a carefully designed protocol, there is just enough structure that the conversation has direction and just enough flexibility that it is writer- and writing-focused. It is important that protocols are used in this way—to support structured feedback without constraining it. I have designed three different protocols for peer feedback that do just that. The first two protocols are for pairs, and the third is for small-group feedback; all are easily accessible for young writers while at the same time helpful in reaching goals. Time and again, when using these protocols, teachers have been astounded by the thoughtful, insightful feedback students offer one another.

Protocol 1: Paired Focus Feedback

This protocol sets up conversation by first having the writer request feedback in specific areas. This, off the bat, sets up a writing focus and sets the scene for the rest of the conversation. Writers can decide to focus on a particular goal and also ask for feedback on qualities of good writing such as focus, voice, elaboration, or a more general focus, like the flow of the piece. The important part here is that writers choose the focus of the feedback they would like to receive. It is simultaneously structured and flexible. One young writer reflected about this protocol: "My partner gave me tips and also gave me a chance to rehearse what I needed to do in my writing. I felt comfortable with this because I knew they wanted to help me and I got to choose what I wanted to talk about." The protocol goes like this:

Partner A: Pick a focus (feedback on a goal, a particular strategy, etc.).

Partner B: Paraphrase the focus for accuracy. "So what you are saying is . . ."

Partners A and B: Place the writing between them and read it together (all or a portion).

Partner B: Offer feedback on the focus. "I noticed . . ." "Here's where . . ." "You might try . . ."

Switch!

Protocol 2: Compare for Feedback

This protocol provides writers with a structure to compare each other's writing and learn from each other. The pair will choose the same focus, such as a similar goal, and compare each other's work on that focus. For example, Marcus and Gil shared a goal of writing an introduction for their argument piece that both hooked the reader and gave background information and context to the rest of the piece. After using the protocol below, Marcus shared, "I realized that I was very factual in my writing and Gil had lots of explanation and not as many facts. I will be adding more explanation and Gil plans on adding more facts."

© Rick Harrington Photography

Partners A and B: Pick a shared focus (can be a similar goal).

Partners A and B: Compare each other's writing, looking for similarities and differences.

Partner A: "What you tried that I'm going to try . . ."

Partner B: "What you tried that I'm going to try . . ."

Protocol 3: Feedback Club

This third protocol is meant for a small group of four or so to gather around one student's piece of writing. That student then receives multiple points of view on different areas of focus. In a nutshell, this protocol begins with one writer choosing a few points of focus, one for each of the partners in his group. This can include his goals and/or other areas of writing on which he may want feedback. I especially like this protocol because writers receive feedback on multiple areas or goals. Other teachers like it as well. Melissa, a middle school teacher, explained: "They were able to share their work with their classmates and also get some self-selected constructive feedback on spelling and grammar, pointing out areas that can be improved in terms of grammar, content, style, or anything else! The students were involved with each other and also learning from one another, even when they were giving, not receiving, feedback." Melissa also shared that her students, once the protocol was learned, easily moved into it without much teacher support and asked to use it often. My favorite part of this protocol is that first the partners write down their feedback on a sticky note, then share their feedback verbally, and finally hand the sticky note over to the writer to use and refer to. Here's how that protocol goes:

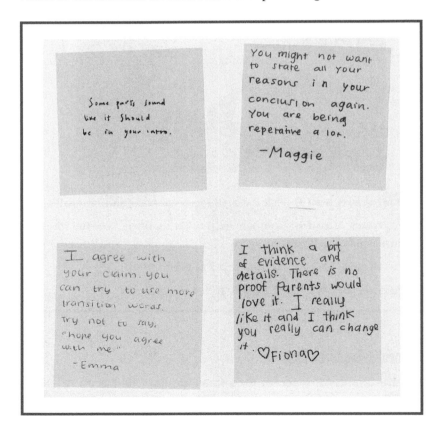

1. Students gather in groups of about four.

2. The lead student chooses the areas in which he or she would like feedback, guided by his or her goals, and asks each writer in the group to take a different focus.

3. The lead student reads the plan, or a portion of the plan (or the draft, or a portion of the draft) aloud while other students write down their feedback on sticky notes.

4. When the lead student is complete, the others, one at a time, share their feedback out loud and then hand the sticky note over to the lead writer to use. They might mirror the teacher's feedback, starting with a strength and suggesting next steps.

Students really took to all three of these protocols, saying, "I learned from my partner, but I also learned more about my writing and myself when I was giving suggestions to my partner." Another writer shared, "I had many new ideas on how to work on the parts of my writing that I needed to revise. Writing alone is a lot more difficult than writing with a friend's advice." Teachers were pleasantly surprised by the students' ability to give one another meaningful feedback, especially in those classrooms that had never used peer feedback.

A few pointers when using these protocols:

1. Model using the protocol so the kids can see how it works. Maybe try modeling a protocol with you and a student in front of the class.

2. Build in time for coaching those partnerships that may need a little extra support.

3. Practice using the protocols over and over again; this will make the protocols feel less like a list of steps and more like a conversation. Eventually, students may not need the protocols at all!

4. Fishbowl (one partnership models for a group) showcasing one group that is making the most of the protocol being discussed. Commentate, like the sportscaster does with tennis, on what is working in this interaction.

Conversations with fellow writers may or may not need a protocol, but planning ahead for those conversations can go a long way. One way to prepare for conversations around goals is for students to pre-plan a few questions based on their goal. Rahim did just that. He started with a few goals, but the one he wanted the most feedback on was "make my story more understandable by elaborating." Knowing he wanted to talk to his partner about this, he designed questions (see below) to get both specific feedback and more general feedback, in a very goal-centered way.

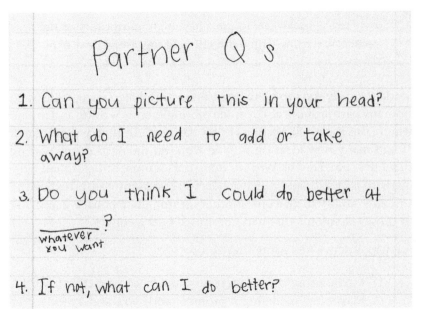

Many students get more out of peer conferring when they frame a few questions about their writing that they want the classmate to address.

Rahim's process was pretty simple here:

1. He thought about the goal on which he wanted the most feedback.

2. He thought, "What questions will give me specific information on my goal?" and wrote a few down.

3. He then thought, "What else do I want feedback on?" and wrote a few down.

4. He met with a partner and used that feedback to revise his thinking and writing.

All in all, peer feedback can be very useful, and when this feedback does not grow organically in a classroom—and it often does not—turning to protocols and preplanning the conversations can go a long way. These experiences can happen on a daily basis, by carving out a few minutes, or they can happen periodically through the week or unit. These conversations may happen spontaneously for particular writers, or as a whole class all at once. It certainly can help us, as the teachers, build in more feedback time when we just cannot meet with everyone we wish. What's more, the student receiving the feedback is not the only one learning. In the small-group protocol, one student remarked, "Even though Carl was not giving feedback on my piece, we were focusing on Ava's piece. Still, this brought up points that I need to focus on in my writing that I hadn't thought about before."

Time is crunched in classrooms, and peer feedback can help, but so can rethinking teacher–student feedback for optimal effectiveness. This next section describes some structures and approaches that teachers can take to giving feedback in efficient and powerful ways.

Teacher Feedback on Goals

I don't think I have ever heard a teacher say "I have plenty of time to teach." Maybe there is someone out there who can say this (lucky teacher!), but the vast majority of teachers are pressed for time. Classrooms today are often overcrowded, and time is so often interrupted by holidays, snow days, sick days, field trips, assemblies, special events, announcements, fire drills, etc. Squeezing in feedback can often feel daunting and frustrating. This section is filled with tips and tools to optimize the feedback time you already have, not only for goal setting but to build in opportunities for feedback of all sorts.

Swift, Sure Structures for Feedback Conversations

Time is on your side—that needs to be your mantra. Even if you can't exactly set an egg timer or your smartphone alarm, you have to be super-aware of the minutes. One reason why it can feel like we don't have enough time for feedback is we spend a long time giving feedback to one student. This is necessary sometimes, but not all of the time. We want to be fair with our time—students who need more support from us should get that support, but not at the expense of the other students. Teachers with whom I work often admit to me that they often don't know how to manage their time well. One way I make my feedback conversations efficient—generally, less than 5 minutes—is by using a structure almost every time I work with a student. This structure gives me a loose plan to follow so I am student-centered and time-efficient. Before I used a structure, my feedback conversations took on a life of their own, meandering down roads that may or may not have been useful, spending so much time with one student that it resembled a tutoring session. The rest of my students missed me and got pretty antsy. Now, with a strong structure, I know the steps I am going to take in giving feedback, and so do the students. A structure is like a route I take in conversation, not unlike my 3-mile walking route. On my walking route, I know each turn I am going to make and approximately how long it will take me. I stick to that route without wandering off course, so I know I am completing what I hoped to and how long it will take me. In that same way, I follow a structure for feedback, so I stay on course.

Similar to the protocols for peer conversation, I chose this structure to create a purposeful, organized conversation that leaves plenty of space for offering feedback that suits the writer in front of me. By following this structure (Anderson, 2000; Calkins et al., 2005; Goldberg & Serravallo, 2007), I make a routine for myself so I can focus my thinking and energy on the feedback I'd like to give. Students also get very used to the structure and expect—and are often prepared for—each part of the conversation, which usually lasts 3 to 7 minutes.

Here is the structure I use most often:

My Structure in Order	Wording I Often Use (I never use everything here)
Ask about the student's goal(s) 1–2 minutes	"What is the goal you are working on?" "What progress have you made?" "What has been challenging?" "Would you show me where you . . . ?" "What's your larger intention in writing?" "What investments have you made?"
Name what is working in reaching that goal 1 minute	"What I am noticing is . . ." "Ways that I see you reaching your goal are . . ." "What seems to be working is . . ." "The steps I see you took are . . ."
Suggest next steps toward reaching that goal 1–2 minutes	"Some next steps are . . ." "You are ready for . . ." "I imagine where you could go next is . . ." "At this point you may want to try . . ."
Optional: Model those next steps 1–2 minutes	"Here's what that can look like . . ." "Watch me as I . . ." "Here's a quick how-to . . ."
Optional: Coach 1–2 minutes	"Want to give it a whirl? I'll stick with you while you do." "Talk through what you are imagining . . ." "What are you going to try first? And then?" [or maybe whisper in quick words of encouragement and advice as the student writes]

This go-to structure for feedback is my foundation. Sometimes I don't need to use all of the parts. For example, if a student seems to grasp the next steps and seemingly can proceed without much support, I may not stay for the coaching time and circle back as a quick check-in. At other points, modeling may not be needed so I will jump right to coaching, or skip coaching altogether as well. I do, however, use the first four steps pretty much every time I give feedback. The big exception is when I can't think of next steps. At that point I will leave the writer with what is working and then spend time thinking about next steps, and if there are any, I will meet with the writer at a later time. I always remind myself that naming strengths is an essential teaching move and if I leave the writer with just that, I still have given powerful feedback.

Your Secret Weapon: Baby Steps Rather Than Big Leaps

You may have noted the time I spend on each part of the conversation. It may feel rushed, especially because I have shared only my words here and not the writer's. One way of keeping to the time and structure is to know that the "next steps" we offer should be lean and concise. Next steps will take a very long time to teach if those steps are big leaps and not baby steps. An example of what I mean by big leaps:

Rashim's Goal	Big Leaps
Make my story more understandable by elaborating.	First, add dialogue. Second, use sensory details to make the setting clear. Third, include inner dialogue. Fourth, reread for clarity.

These are large concepts that take a whole lot of explaining, especially if the writer is just learning how to use them. Choosing just one, or a part of one, is more like a baby step. For example, we may suggest just adding dialogue and then show the steps to do that:

Baby Steps for Rashim to Add Dialogue

1. Picture your story in your head, like a film.
2. Imagine hearing the characters talk.
3. Find that part in your story.
4. Write the words in quotations.
5. Reread for clarity.

A few more big leaps whittled down to baby steps:

If the Student's Goal Is . . .	A Big Leap Suggestion Would Be . . .	A Baby Step Suggestion or Strategy Would Be . . .
Bring in expert voices to defend my claim.	Research in valid online sources, paraphrasing or quoting as needed. Cite the source using MLA format.	Paraphrase it into your own words by: 1. Reading a portion of the text. 2. Covering with your hand and saying out loud, in your own words, that idea or concept. Try this a few different ways. 3. Writing down your favorite phrasing.
Stick to a theme in my fiction piece, revealing it slowly throughout the story.	Decide on a theme and incorporate symbolism, flashback, and a character's inner growth throughout the story.	Use flashback by: 1. Imagining you are the character and what just happened to you reminds you of an earlier memory. 2. Picturing that memory in your mind like a series of snapshots, rehearsing it in your head a few times. 3. Thinking to yourself, "Does this memory give my reader more important information about my character? Does it shed some light on the theme?" If so, write it down.
Structure my informational book so that it best teaches the reader about my topic.	Use paragraphs, transitional language, headings, subheadings, and graphics.	Use paragraphs to: 1. Read over your writing. 2. Think, "Where do I switch to another idea?" and "Where does my reader need a little brain break?" 3. Start a new paragraph at those spots by indenting.

I am sure there are others who can make it work with larger groups, but I find it more useful, both for myself and the students, to keep the groups to four or less. If I have more than four ready for the same feedback, I teach to the same goal two separate times.

Keeping a structure can really help make feedback conversations efficient and effective. So can working with small groups of writers working toward the same goals.

Time Savers: Small Groups With Similar Goals

Teaching in small groups is another way to make the most of the time crunch in classrooms.

One way to create these small groups is to gather students who have similar goals. Again, working with a small group can take up a huge amount of time without a strong structure to follow. I usually follow the structure for one-on-one conversations with small tweaks for the number of students, and these usually last about 10 minutes or so. The first thing I do is leave out the first section completely—the one about asking questions about the goal—and gather information about goals prior to the small-group session. I may do this by observing writers at work, reading some of their writing, or asking questions directly. Once I have decided on who belongs in the small group, I follow this structure:

My Structure in Order	Wording I Often Use (I never use everything here)
Name for the writers what is working in reaching that goal 1–2 minutes	"What I am noticing with all of you is . . ." "Ways that I see all of you reaching your goals are . . ." "What seems to be working is . . ."
Suggest next steps toward that goal 1–2 minutes	"Together, you may take these next steps . . ." "You are all ready for . . ." "At this point you may all want to try . . ." "Because you have . . . you are ready to . . ."
Optional: Model those next steps 2–3 minutes	"Here's what that can look like . . ." "Watch me as I . . ." "Here's a quick how-to . . ."
Optional: Coach, one at a time 2–4 minutes	"Can we start with you? Let's try out loud . . ." "I'm just going to watch and whisper in while you write . . ."

To clarify, the coaching part of the structure is the time to individu-alize a bit. Imagine at this point the students try out what you just modeled. Take a minute or two to adjust, as needed, what you mod-eled for each student, providing individualized feedback. I find that this is always needed—since all writers are different, all writers use feedback in slightly adjusted ways. These moments of support can go a long way in creating the independence writers need in working with those next steps on their own. Sometimes I even like to jot on a sticky note or ask students to jot on the feedback tracker (see Chapter 1) the main points of the small-group learning time. These may be the steps of the model/demo, a small reminder, or commitment the writer makes in response to the feedback.

One-on-one and small-group feedback are, in my experience, opti-mal, though they are not always possible. We often need to give writ-ten feedback and, of course, not the "red-pen" kind of feedback we explored in Chapter 1. Let's move on, then, to exploring some ways of using written feedback to support writers in reaching their goals.

Tips for Squeezing in as Much Face-to-Face Feedback as Possible

Tip 1: Move on and come back.

Sometimes face-to-face conversations become lengthy when we are watching writers try the next steps we just modeled. It is okay to walk away while they try these next steps, meet with another student, and then circle back to see how it went. Do this when you think, even a little bit, that they don't need too much coaching to try it out.

Tip 2: Use the "waiting" minutes.

There are always those minutes when we are waiting to transition to or from someplace—the last minutes of class, an assembly, lunch. These may be moments we use for checking in on goals. What is the goal you are working on? How is it going? What progress have you made? What has been challenging? And maybe, "I have some ideas for that. Let's catch up."

(Continued)

(Continued)

Tip 3: When you can, have writers write in class, at least periodically.

If you are in a setting where writing does not happen on a daily basis inside the four walls of your classroom, or if most of the writing is done at home, consider building in time to write under your gaze every so often. This way you can gather information not only about the writing but the writers and their process. This can also help you give face-to-face feedback every so often.

Tip 4: Set yourself a goal to trim.

Sometimes face-to-face feedback is happening every day but only one or two writers are receiving that feedback because the conversations go so long. Maybe set yourself a goal to follow a particular structure (like the one above) and pace yourself to fit that structure into a few minutes less than you might normally spend. If your conferences are 15 minutes long, shoot for 12 minutes instead. Keep paring down the time until you are able to fit in more conversations.

Designing Written Feedback

In many cases, writers will receive written feedback more often than they will face-to-face feedback. There are many perks to written feedback. First, the writer can refer back to it again and again. I personally use the notes left for me about my writing almost like a checklist of small goals for myself. I read them over and refer back to them often. I keep them in mind as I revise and also as I compose new writing. Another perk of written feedback is the power it has on the writer. When written in a way that acknowledges and encourages the writer within and gives some advice, encouragement, and/or ideas about the writing itself, written feedback holds the potential to empower the writer.

On the flip side, written feedback can also do a number on the writer. Written feedback can potentially sting if not intentionally crafted to do otherwise. It also has a tendency to be overlooked by young writers, especially when there is too much of it or it takes on an exclusively corrective, red-pennish approach (see Chapter 1 for more on this concept). Written feedback, especially in its most useful form, can also take a long time to write. It is much quicker and often easier to jump into a piece and correct it ourselves. However, this does not necessarily offer actionable feedback. Let's explore a quick, useful structure for written feedback that can be both empowering and efficiently written. Let's do this by studying two examples of feedback from Pam.

To add some context to this first example of written feedback, the writer is spending a few days exploring ideas for an information piece but has not yet chosen one. In this case, she is considering the possibility of writing all about Rick Riordan's *Percy Jackson* series by quickly drafting how it might go. Pam keeps this in mind and offers a two-part feedback approach—first, naming strengths and then suggesting, or in this case implying, next steps. 👜 ♥ ◎ 🏛

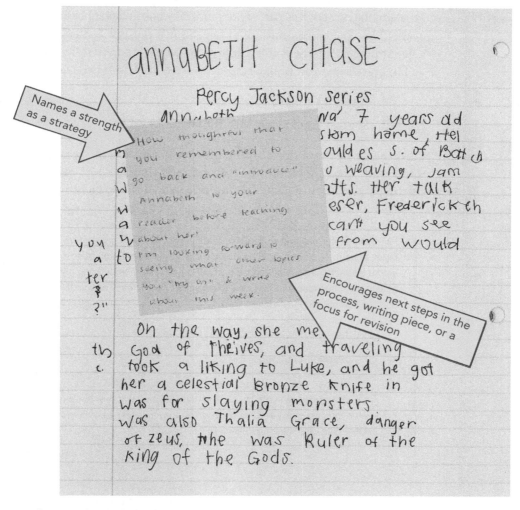

We all want to be Maxwell Perkinses to our F. Scott Fitzgeralds and write lengthy feedback that prepares our writers for greatness! But the reality is—we don't have time. Pam's two-part feedback, written on a sticky note, supports the writer by noticing a strength and then recasting it as a strategy for the writer to keep honing.

Within these two parts, Pam has included some other qualities as well. First, when she names the strength, she does so in a way that identifies the strategy that this young author used: "introducing the character to the reader." When Pam names this as a strategy and a strength, it supports the writer in using this same strategy in future writing. In the second part of her feedback, Pam encourages and points toward next steps. Pam could have easily suggested a little less "getting to know" the character, or some "brevity of sentence" work, or "let's get to the topic sentence early on." Instead, Pam chooses to support this writer in truly making the most of this part of the process by encouraging her to explore other ideas before committing to one. So it is not just a strength–next step structure Pam uses—it is a little more detailed than that. To simplify a bit, one way we can think about written feedback is in two parts:

1. Name a strength as a strategy

2. Suggest a next step with the writer in mind

Either one of these steps can be used by itself and still be brief and powerful. Take a look at how Pam implied that the goal below was strong by suggesting next steps for one part of the student's goal.

> My goal for informational writing is to make a lead that gets my readers ready to learn. I will take small steps, one chapter at a time, and try to ignore distractions as best I can. It is important to remember to keep my goal in mind because that way I will know what I would like to accomplish, and I will be more determined to finish it.
>
> Feb 4, 9:11am Reply

> **Pamela Koutrakos**
>
> I bet we can look to mentor texts to get lots of different ideas for how our openings might go. I love getting inspired by other authors (students, my own peers, and also published authors). Let's study interesting openings together!
>
> Feb 4, 9:11am Reply

In all the feedback we give, the words we choose need to be pitched toward action, next steps, forward movement. The writer should feel sanctioned for the effort of his current piece, and yet most of all, motivated and focused for future work as a writer.

Techy Goal Setting

Here are two ways of using technology for goal setting and feedback.

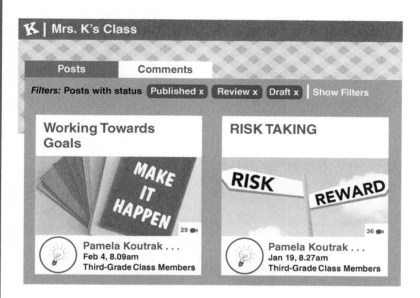

Image sources: Stacked fanned paper courtesy of Pixabay/Counselling; lightbulb and signs courtesy of clipart.com

Blogs

Pam's comments were in response to goals students wrote on her blog. Both the teacher and the students can respond in supporting those goals.

	Commitment
Aman	Redo first paragraph
April	Add info to shock the reader to draw them in.
Carl	In my orienting paragraph I'm going to mention my 3 reasons.
Cathy	Keeping my point and idea across my paragraph by using the right TE and thoughts
Ellie	Work on orienting the reader and teir two words
Emma	Finish my flash draft of my first paragraph tying in 2 pieces of evidence
Greg	Finish my flash draft of my first paragraph tying in 2 pieces of evidence
Janet	Go back to my first pararaph and see what I could improve.
Kate	Today I am going to put cohesion in my 2 paragraph
Leo	Think of cohesion as a gift and oppertunity
Lionel	make my body of the essay and include text evidence and quotes to soport the idea.
Loreni	Today I am going to finish another paragraph and go back to other paragraph and add more.
Lucio	Check over my orientation paragraph and make sure it has everything I wanted it to have
Marianne	Make sure that I have not repeated anything in my flash drive and adding higher level words.
Mrs. Sarsten	Incorporating powerful tone through word choice
Nester	Edit first paragraph to make it the best it can be
Noen	Finish flash draft and really explain the best reason with a lot of text and since this is the 1st one.
Rafiq	I will reread my drcaft and will try to switch low level words with teir 2 words.
Sabah	Edit first paragraph and finish so I can go onto paragraph 2
Saif	Find 2 pieces of evidence ot support my first reason.

Google Forms

Laura takes a moment as a one-to-one school to use Google forms for daily commitments. Before setting off to work, every student jots their commitment for their work.

Most important, the flavor of written feedback is one that empowers writers through strengths and next steps. It does not do the work for the writer but rather supports the writer just enough with a direction toward her goal.

When we cultivate ownership of learning in our writers, they feel freer to seek out inspiration and discover goals from published authors as well as peers.

Wrapping It Up

As we conclude the chapter on goal setting, when writers look to stretch and grow, we will move on to explore other impactful, important, and untraditional ways of supporting students' writing and writing identity. Our next stop is feedback, when we are looking to support ownership and agency: choice making.

Chapter 6

When Writers Need Ownership and Agency
Feedback to Support Choice Making

Choice is central to agency. Making a choice requires one to act—
preferably to deliberate and act.

—Peter Johnston

Picture for a moment the disengaged writers with whom you have worked. Maybe their heads are on their desks, they're doodling rather than writing, or they're getting up to take their fifth bathroom break. I picture Jeff, a sixth grader who used to gaze at the ceiling or pretend to write, or cope by distracting others. And Sarah, whose hand was always in the air, waiting for me to help. Lots of raised hands, lots of blank pages at the end of a 45-minute writing period. Sometimes it feels like many of our writers are waiting and waiting and waiting rather than writing and writing and writing—waiting for directions on what to do next, or waiting for your approval before taking the next step.

As a teacher, these disengaged writers would make me go into this earnest overdrive, and I'd pull out all the stops with enticing sentence starters, pep talks, and even stickers. Just as I did, and with the best of intentions, many teachers whose classrooms I visit offer an incredible amount of support in the form of prompts, graphic organizers, checklists, one-on-one conversations, writing formulas, lists of grammar rules to follow, and more. While many of these supports can be helpful to a writer, they can also backfire. In this chapter, we'll explore why, but here's a spoiler alert: These supports often don't work because they perpetuate dependence. So the million-dollar question you need to ask yourself when you step in to support a disengaged writer is this: How much ownership is actually in the student's hands? How much am I truly turning over to the student here?

Let's take the use of graphic organizers as an example. These organizers can be a supportive tool and can help writers plan their writing, especially when students can choose the organizer that best fits their potential writing piece. Organizers, however, can also become more of a crutch than a tool. For example, if writers are required to use a graphic organizer that is chosen by the teacher at the onset of every writing piece (often a different organizer each time), the writer may begin to believe a few things:

- Before writing, I must be provided with a planning tool.
- My teacher knows the right way to plan my writing. I don't.
- There is a different way of planning for every writing piece, and it's a mystery until the graphic organizer is revealed.
- Writing is a school task.

Used without ownership, a graphic organizer can end up hindering writers' learning and growth. As teachers, we need to be super-intentional in how we introduce and use this and other tools over time. The adage "variety is the spice of life" is apt here; I like to suggest to teachers that they offer more than one tool or technique for structuring writing, do brief demonstrations of how each might be used—*but then leave it to the writer to select one that suits*. I'm being deliberately general in using the term *suits* because I've found that what appeals to a student writer on any given day is quirky, not predictive of what might work for him or her next, and that's okay. To engage each writer, we have to embrace student choice, and not overthink it. The choice alone builds agency.

A Need for Choice, Now

Now, let me get on my soapbox: "Choice-less" writing approaches are wrecking kids with prompts, rules, and mandatory structures— 12 years of that and most students don't find the way to their own voice and originality. This is a national blight, because a lack of originality isn't just a matter of fewer future novelists and screen-writers—it's symptomatic of a society whose students aren't being cultivated for the creative thinking they are going to need in any field of endeavor. Choice-less writing approaches drive our disengaged writers to give up on themselves, but even our capable students despair. Seventh grader Sophia lamented, "I love to write. I just wish I had teachers who let me take risks and make some of my own choices. But in writing, you have to read the teacher's mind. I find a lot of kids don't even try. The only thing we have been given since I was in first grade was the same structure over and over again. One time I tried to add my own ideas and I got a failing grade." For the sake of all writers, writing instruction must evolve away from prompts, "red-pen" approaches, a hyperfocus on writing rules and single-minded structures, and instead make it truly okay to be original in one's writing. What happens as a result? The writing identity and originality flourish, and these "rising tides" lift all boats, because writing "skills" and student performance on standardized tests ascend as well.

In this chapter I share approaches to engage those disinterested writers in ways that support them to take ownership of their writing, to shed dependency, and to become stronger, invested, more passionate, original writers. First, though, let's tease out some finer definitions of originality, ownership, and agency.

Originality, Ownership, and Agency

To me, originality is a quality that arises when a writer's work is aligned with the writer's being. You read it and you know it's spot-on "his" of "hers," unique as a fingerprint. To write with a quest for originality—let's think of it as a verb—a writer gathers ideas and composes in a way that gets him closer to true uniqueness. The writer feels free to bring herself to the page, in content, style, and voice. Now, as you read on, keep this in mind: *Ownership and agency lead to originality, and originality feeds ownership and agency.*

Ownership in writing, as I define it, is a state of mind. It comes from a writer's belief that her writing is actually hers—it's a sense of belonging and relationship between the writer and her writing. The writer *claims* her writing as her own and holds a sense of responsibility for this writing. Writers who possess ownership accept feedback and interpret how to use (or not use) that feedback. By contrast, if students think of writing as a series of assignments to complete and not something they, themselves, create, they do not own their writing. If they think of writing exclusively as a task to finish for the teacher, not a powerful use of their voice, they are lacking ownership. They may not identify themselves as a writer but rather as a task completer. What's more, our most disengaged writers are not the only students who feel a lack of ownership. Many students at varying levels of engagement may or may not own their writing. Some other signals of "disownership":

Common Signs of "Disownership"

- A sense of going through the motions without engagement
- Quick completion of writing without a willingness to revise
- Unfinished writing
- A multitude of spelling, punctuation, and clarity inaccuracies
- Extra-large type and wide margins
- All feedback is ignored unless it helps the student finish faster

Ownership does not necessarily mean that writers actually do something with their writing—that's where the concept of agency steps in. Taking action as an outgrowth of ownership is agency. Ownership and agency make a mighty pairing! Agency "refers to the thoughts and actions taken by people that express their individual power" (Cole, 2015). Agency is ownership in motion—it is the actions taken by the writer to write with intention. Agency is also a tell-tale sign of a strong writing identity. Peter Johnston, in *Choice Words* (2004), explores this notion of agency in literacy, stating it "is not only central for the individual's sense of competence and well-being, and for his or her performance, but also indispensable for democratic living" (p. 41).

Common Signs of Ownership and Agency in Writing

- The writer seeks out specific feedback from teachers and peers
- Feedback is carefully considered and used when the writer sees it fits
- The writer holds a sense of investment and commitment to his writing
- Writing is heavily revised and often reworked completely
- Time is well utilized
- The writer may seem lost in her work

How, then, can we support writers in ownership and agency? We can offer choice as a form of feedback. This is a concept that takes a moment to sink in: *choice as a form of feedback.*

"Choice is central to agency" (Johnston, p. 36). Making choices engages and empowers the writer and strengthens the writer's identity. If we want writing to be powerful, then we want to support writers' ownership and agency by making space for writerly actions and choices.

Choice not only fosters ownership and agency, it also has the potential to create a community of writers whose identity and writing are strong. Johnston also insists that creating a sense of agency as a class-room community "offers the possibility of developing an identity through affiliation" (p. 36). In other words, if all students possess ownership and agency through choice making, the collective writing identity is strengthened, and by design the individual is as well. After all, Johnston continues, "children grow into the intellectual life around them" (p. 36).

Choice can be built into instruction and feedback quite often throughout each writing experience. Let's consider Laura Sarsten's classroom. She offers writerly choice in small and large ways by weaving choice into the fabric of her teaching. In both whole-group instruction and small-group/one-on-one feedback, Laura leaves the choice up to the student. This may come in the form of questions: "Where will you be working today to keep yourself focused on your writing?" or "What commitments will you make to your goal today?" Choice also may

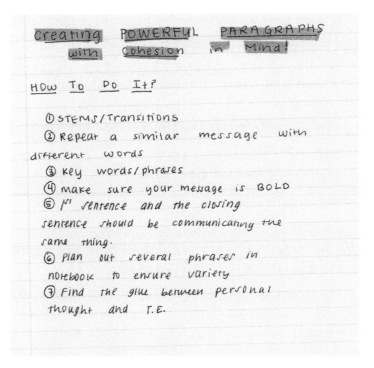

Even when we want our students to try particular craft techniques, we can offer a significant degree of choice.

come in the form of a list of techniques that students can refer to as they make writing choices (see the previous example). Laura projects this list from her notebook under the document camera and students choose from this list as they write and revise. *There is not an expectation that all of these techniques are used, just those that the writer sees fit.*

I took some time to talk to Laura's students about having so many choices as writers. One student, Rohan, shared that having choices in writing makes his ideas fit better: "Some structures don't work with some ideas. Having a choice in structure makes my ideas clearer." Another student, Libby, offered: "I am able to make choices because my teacher trusts me." (This particular comment bowled me over, and compelled me to deepen my thinking about the link between choice and trust, which I will explore a bit later in this chapter.) Naturally, you may be thinking, should teachers *really* trust students to make their own choices? Research suggests we should.

Research Support

Choice is a powerful thing in classrooms. According to Alfie Kohn in his article "Choices for Children: Why and How to Let Students Decide" (1993), "at least one study has found that children given more 'opportunity to participate in decisions about schoolwork' score higher on standardized tests; other research shows that they are more likely than those deprived of autonomy to continue working even on relatively uninteresting tasks. There is no question about it: even if our only criterion is academic performance, choice works." Educator and author Amanda Ronan (2015) writes in her post "7 Ways to Hack Your Classroom to Include Student Choice" that "the psychological effects of feeling a sense of control are well-documented and include greater levels of happiness and activity, and lower levels of stress and anxiety. Educational research has shown that choice leads to more confident, more capable, and more interested students." All of these outcomes are just what we wish for in our classrooms—successful, happy, engaged writers. "Choice is where it starts for reluctant writers, and if we want them to warm up to writing, we need to structure our classes so that our students have some say in what they write" (Gallagher, 2006, p. 91).

Just a Few Outcomes of Choice Making in the Classroom

- Lower stress levels

- Higher test scores

- Perseverance through hard or uninteresting experiences

- Student autonomy, agency, and ownership

- Confident, capable, and interested students

What I Observed in Classrooms Filled With Choice

- Teachers are often pleasantly surprised by what the writers do

- Anchor charts that give options for choices

- Partnership conversations with a loose, guided structure for those conversations

- Student talk and writing outweigh teacher talk and modeling

- Teachers use the choices writers make as whole-class lessons

- Writing materials are nearby that students can use without asking

- Teachers model their own choices and their choice-making process

- Teachers do not write on student writing; any changes are made by the writers themselves

- There is a low hum of activity

- When writers get distracted, they pull themselves and others back into focus

- When giving feedback, writers offer choices to fellow writers: "You could try . . ." or "You could try . . ."

The Trust Fall of Developing Writers

Let's circle back to Libby's instructive words about Laura's choice-filled classroom: "I am able to make choices because my teacher trusts me." Libby's words really got me thinking and researching. I wondered if trust is the key that opens the first "door" that leads to a writer's effective choice making, which in turn opens a second "door" to ownership and agency. I decided to study other classrooms where ownership and agency were evident through this lens of trust. When looking at classrooms from this point of view, I learned that, yes, trust seemed to make all of the difference. In the classrooms where ownership and agency are present, the teacher explicitly and implicitly shares that she or he trusts the students to make choices and the students trust the teacher right back.

© Rick Harrington Photography

Trust in our students is an identical twin to an investment in knowing our students. They are look-alike mindsets. Thus, it shouldn't surprise us that trust is also vital to building a writer's identity. Ben Johnson in his Edutopia blog, Developing Students' Trust: The Key to a Learning Partnership, writes: "As students get older, they often trust less. Most students will take what we offer but will not allow a learning partnership because they do not trust us. Unless they trust us, they are unapproachable." Without that learning partnership, we cannot make the inroads to supporting the writer's identity and growth. Therefore, when we consider the concept of trust, we are not only talking about a teacher trusting a writer to make choices, we are also talking about the student believing the teacher, or trusting the teacher right back. In other words, does the student believe that the teacher trusts her? In John Hattie's words (2012), "Trust means students seeing that the teacher believes in them—especially when they are struggling" (p. 158). Trust, of course, is a two-way street. Let's explore a few ways that we build trust in the classroom where the teacher and the student hold mutual trust.

Language That Fosters Trust

- How do you plan to solve that problem?
- What can I do to help?
- What's your plan?
- One strategy that may help you is . . .
- I have faith in you.
- I trust you.
- Maybe talk to a partner for more support with that . . .
- Would you talk to another writer who can learn from your process? It will help him make some informed choices.
- Here are some options. Which one do you want to try?
- Have a go at it and see what happens.
- You may want to start with . . .
- It sounds like your focus is . . . Let's talk through some next steps . . .
- You have so many different directions you can go in . . .
- The more ideas the better. It gives you options . . .
- Maybe consider . . .
- The choice is yours . . .

 Available for download at **http://resources.corwin.com/McGee-Feedback**

While we know that trust is pivotal, it is often tricky. It is sometimes easier to hold onto a distrust of students because of past experiences or because of a single student in the class.

In fact, how we respond when students give us reasons not to trust can make us more or less trustworthy. When we give up on trusting our writers, they give up on trusting us. This is not to say that we don't respond to the writers in our classroom who have made us feel we can't trust; we just do so while holding steady in the belief that writers can make writerly choices to develop ownership and agency. For example, when teachers Courtney Rejent and Lena Guroian had a student who did not focus on writing when it was writing time, who, when their back was turned, was distracting others, their response to him was clear: This was not the way things work in this classroom. They both quickly addressed the lack of engagement and the distraction by being steadfast in their belief that they could trust this student, despite the fact that he had just proven differently. They reminded him of his role and responsibilities as a writer and asked what he and they could do to help him refocus. What they did not do was sacrifice trust by taking away choice.

The research on trust is clear: Trust is not built in a single moment but many small moments, over time (Brown, 2015; Gottman, 2011). There are a few ways we can collect these trust-building moments to show writers that we trust them to make writerly choices. Brené Brown (2015) details in *The Anatomy of Trust* that trust is built through reliability. Writers will trust us if we stay consistent with our actions around choice, ownership, and agency, and we in turn will learn to trust students to make writerly choices. One way to build trust is to expect (and allow) choice making throughout the process, not just in, say, coming up with ideas or choosing where to work that day. We show reliability when we consistently support students in making their own choices by offering a menu of possibilities. This may include different choices on how to structure sentences, how and when to use different verb tenses, a few ways of taking risks or setting goals or reflecting, options on choosing where to paragraph, or possibilities in research techniques (much more on this later in the chapter).

We can also build trust by consistently giving a particular type of feedback, just as Courtney does:

> My students know that I do not look for their mistakes, but I value what they are writing. I show that by asking them about their writing formally, as in conferences, but sometimes it is in the hallway or in between classes. They also feel my trust because I notice and compliment when they take risks or try something new. I do not compliment them

only when they are compliant with something I asked them to do. My students know that I trust them because even on polished pieces, I label the places in their pieces where they found successes and I don't "correct" their papers for them. In this mindset, I honor every word they wrote. They trust me as much as I trust them.

Trust is built through reliability and consistency—by showing writers day in and day out that we trust them to make choices.

Building in Choice as Part of Feedback

Offering choice is a technique we can use when giving feedback—a sophisticated and trusting technique and not one we would choose in every feedback exchange, but as often as possible. Offering choice as a form of feedback allows the students to decide their own next steps with guidance. When we build in choice, ownership and agency strengthen. It is a win–win.

There are countless ways to build in choices throughout the writing time, and we will spend the rest of the chapter exploring ways of offering choice as a form of feedback. We will begin with four moves you can make to build choice into any day. From there we will get even more practical and consider choices we can offer in research for writing, structure, elaboration, and grammar (yes, grammar!).

Four Ways to Advance Choice Making Every Day

Here are four ways I give student writers the feedback that I expect and trust their independence:

1. Write the write: Like the mantra "you gotta walk the walk," you gotta model choice making. Courtney and Lena, those teachers who give students the chance to make choices, also routinely demonstrate their choice-making process. In this particular lesson, Courtney and Lena modeled how they dig back into their research to begin selecting topics for their research paper. Courtney had her research notebook in hand and showed the writers, step by step, how she works through the selection process. Lena created a chart of Courtney's process, adding some tips and pointers along the way.

At the end of the lesson, they turned over the choice to the students. When students had difficulty, Lena and Courtney coached the students through the process. Never once did they take the choice-making process out of the writers' hands, even when the students had difficulty. In the end, everyone had at least a few ideas of where they wanted to go in their writing. Many learned, through the choice-making process, that the topic they thought they wanted to write about was not a good choice for them—an important decision best made early on in the writing process.

2. **Practice a little archery:** It's somewhat counterintuitive, but to cultivate freedom and agency in our writers, sometimes we have

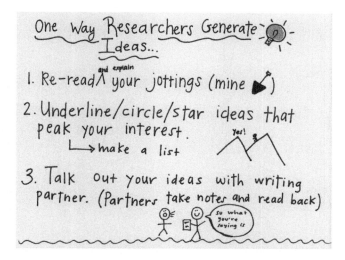

Model for students how you make choices in order to be productive as a writer.

To model any choice-making process, follow a few simple steps:

1. Think about the choices you want your writers to make that day.

2. Try it out yourself first or imagine what you would do to make those choices.

3. Jot down the steps you took.

4. Share those steps with your students.

to get them to take aim and hit the bull's eye on what it is they are shooting for that day. We need them to name their intention. Otherwise (to belabor this metaphor!) writers can have arrows flying every which way for days on end. To encourage choice, use questions to root out the goals your students set. Begin or end writing time with the questions: *What are you going to commit to today to help you reach your goal? What are your next steps [for homework or the next class period] toward your goal?* Students can then either talk or jot about those choices and then act upon them. This is a simple yet powerful way of tying goal setting and choice making together. See the notebook entry below.

Notice the "baby steps" of daily goals. Slow and steady win the race.

3. **Select the spa music setting:** It's all in how you say it, right? If we want our students to be relaxed rather than anxious so they can *apply* what we say, each word and rise and fall of our voice counts. Agency is acting upon ownership, and writers can't act or think well when they are holding their breath, waiting for corrections. When you meet with a writer face to face, remember that the best questions hold a tone that you are there to support the writer, not to fix anything. Sometimes we might start by asking if it is a good time to talk, and if not, when would be? I have found this approach to be especially helpful in resistant writers or resistant talkers. They feel much more comfortable when we can agree upon a good stopping point for feedback. Other effective questions follow.

Questions That Support Ownership and Agency

- What's working well right now in your writing?

- What is tricky that I can help you with today?

- What are some choices you have made today? How have they worked out?

- How can I help?

- What sort of feedback would be most useful right now?

- How can you solve that problem?

- What might you do next?

4. **Hand over the keys, really:** Yup. Like when you first let your toddler pour milk from a big carton into a small cup or allowed your teenager to get behind the wheel with you in the car, life is one big trust fall, huh? As teachers, we may have a wee tendency to *want* to play air-traffic controller to a couple dozen others every day, so all the more reason to step way back. Let students create their own choices. Ask students to create their own choices. Often. For example, Pam Koutrakos's students often collect a bunch of different possibilities

for themselves before selecting one to go with. They may collect a bunch of writing ideas from which to choose. Or they may write a number of different leads and pick their favorite. They may rewrite an awkwardly worded sentence over and over and choose the one that works best. They simply create choice-making opportunities for themselves.

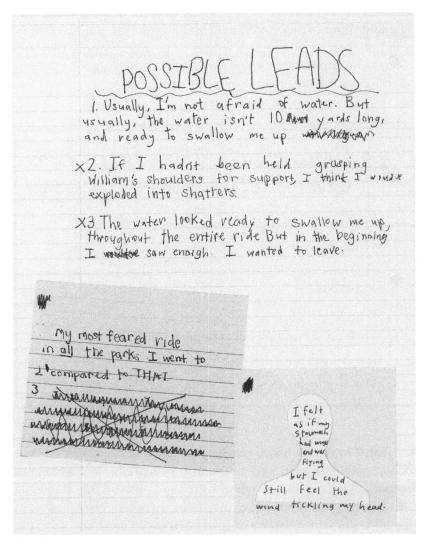

When we ask students to generate choices, and we do this often, it becomes a habit. The habit not only develops agency in writers, but enlivens creativity and problem solving too.

Feedback That Offers Choices in Research Writing

Research is a place where reading and writing coincide. Strong informational and argument writing springs from a strong collection of research. In my personal experience as a middle grade and even high school student, there was only one way I was permitted to research, and that was using index cards in a plastic box. I had to write one fact per index card and then organize the cards by subtopic. I can see the logic in the system, but I can tell you it did not work for me—I somehow inevitably lost many index cards and my grades suffered because of this, probably because my research was thin and sketchy. I am so happy that today I can research using digital tools because I cannot lose them the way I lost my index cards—it fits my research style much better.

Research is not a one-size-fits-all approach. One way to support ownership and agency in writing is by offering choices of research-collecting tools. Writers can choose the type of research tools that best help them not only collect information but also think deeply about their research to strengthen the writing to come. Courtney and Lena offered a variety of note-taking structures and supported students in choosing which tool worked best. On the next page is their anchor chart. While the students used these choices, they were also encouraged to use self-created tools if they fit better. Courtney and Lena introduced each note-taking structure by modeling how they used them in their own personal research topic.

On pages 181–182 are two samples of two different students' research. Notice the different styles of note-taking. Even though their styles were different, both writers shared that by choosing the note-taking tool, they were able to grow their thinking about their topic.

Larry, the writer of the sample on page 181, has a more flexible style of taking notes, feeling almost like a flowchart of information and ideas. Sarah, the writer featured on page 182, has a more organized, systematic, color-coded style. Danny described his research and note-taking style this way: "It helps me with my ideas. I can analyze the research—and this text was really complex—so I was able to really understand it. It also gives me more ideas." Sarah said: "Choosing my own note-taking structure makes research easier.

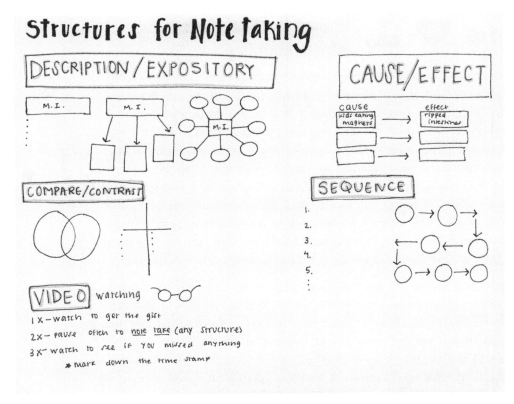

Courtney and Lena, for their research papers, encouraged students to choose their own topics. The topics their writers chose to research were both sophisticated and varied. Talking with these students, I was impressed by their passion and investment in their topics—a reason also to allow choice in topic selection when possible. Topics included:

- Reality TV: Is It Real?
- The Pros and Cons of Technology Today
- The History of Nike Sneakers
- Military Weapons From WWII Through Today
- Mediums and the Sixth Sense
- Stress and Middle Schoolers

I know what I still want to learn. Without the choice, research is harder, more confusing. I feel like I am now an expert."

Offering choice in research collection is a simple yet highly effective approach to creating ownership and agency in writers of informational and argument writing. Once this research is complete, writers will need some options on structures, because that too is not a one-size-fits-all approach.

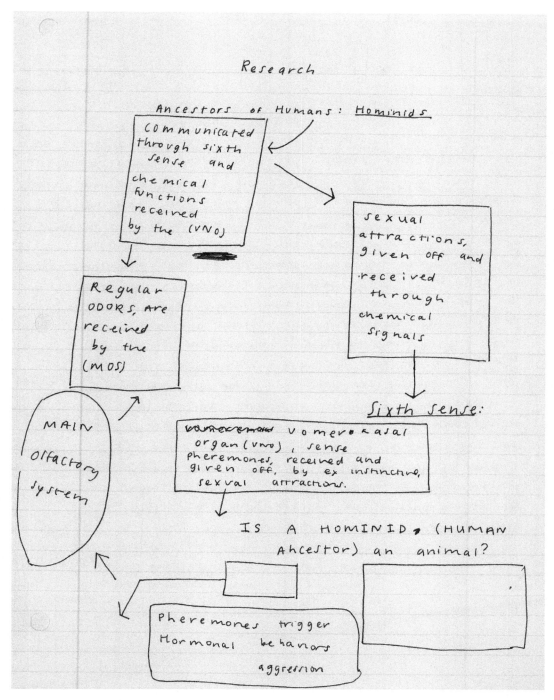

There is actually a creativity to note-taking, especially when it maps the thinking process of the writer.

Red
Pink
Blue
Green

4 - Boxes
4 - colors

using different
colors.

Young children get stressed out because their parents are over schooling their kids, having them being ~~toff~~ and have tantrums, maybe they aren't getting enough sleep the amount they should get is 9-11 hours for 6-12 years old. Not talking to them because your busy with your job or many min their parent   or got sick.

Jotting 4 box jot
Older children get stress as well like they aren't making themselves to bussy or over scheduling themselves, Also they should have 8 ½ or 9 ½ hours of sleep because they need this to have a good mood but also they need adolescents for their body. They also need this to grow and get taller and get a growths spert so they can have developed muscles.

All ages adults & kids get stressed in school some things that they can do is examine the testing, homework, and final exam policies. Another strategy is to stop publishing the high honor / honor in the school newspaper. Also getting extra help in a subject is a strategy that might help your stress decrease and get BETTER.

And for all off the ages of childern look at how you define success and how to communicate that your child is OK. Limit media time and Increase family time, especially eat meals together as a family or go on family trips with no technology. Also the biggest thing that's causing stress is phones, Ipads and more modern technology.

When students' notebook entries reflect the choices they've made, it gives teachers so much more to talk about during face-to-face meetings.

Feedback That Offers Choices in Text Structure

The subject of structure in writing tends to be a touchy one, I have noticed. Most agree that writing needs structure, yet how to approach structure is often hotly debated. The debate often centers around the five paragraph essay—the staple of many schools. Within the five paragraph essay are, of course, five paragraphs: the first is an introduction, followed by three supporting paragraphs, and then a concluding paragraph. Each paragraph has a topic sentence followed by three supporting details, followed by a concluding sentence (see the Feedback That Offers Choices in Grammar and Conventions section for more on sentence structure). Often this structure is used like a formula into which writers plug words, and the outcome is a piece of well-organized writing. This approach may vary a bit by adding a few more paragraphs to the body, or starting with a three paragraph essay structure, but it is still the same basic premise.

While I don't disagree that writing needs structure—structure is, after all, a quality of good writing—I do think that structure should be chosen at the service of the writer and her bigger purpose and meaning. Writers use structure to organize their thinking and express themselves with clarity. However, when structure becomes *the* most important part of writing, writers lose ownership, agency, and choice. They work to input words into the structure rather than make thoughtful, writerly choices. Kimberly Hill Campbell in *Beyond the Five Paragraph Essay* (2014) writes, "Often, the formula becomes a stopping point instead of a starting point. Its emphasis on organization over content squelches complex ideas that do not fit neatly into three boxes" (p. 62). Strictly speaking, if we do not offer some choice in structure, students' ownership and agency suffer.

When we do offer choices in structure, pretty amazing work starts to happen. Notice I am not arguing that we remove structure from writing instruction; I am proposing that we approach structure with choices. To make these choices especially useful for writers, it may be helpful to model how to choose a structure (we will look at the many structural possibilities in just a bit). Let's start with informational writing. You may want to start by studying different text structures in informational writing in a few model texts so writers are a bit familiar with them.

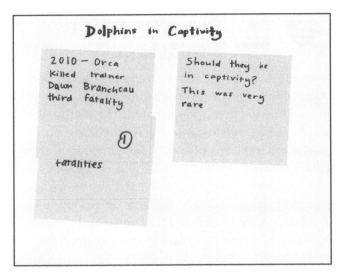

Once students were familiar with the structures often found in informational text, I modeled how to choose a structure using the pages and chart below. In these first side-by-side pages, I thought it would be effective to set them up using the compare-and-contrast structure. The topic was dolphins, and I wanted to compare how humans treat dolphins in

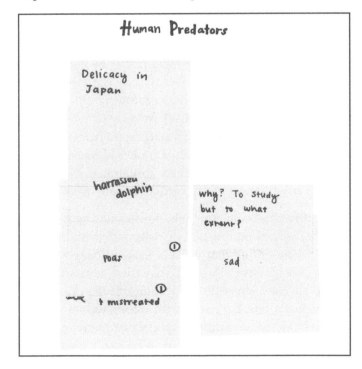

the wild versus how dolphins treat humans when they are in captivity. I chose this structure to highlight how cruel humans can be and how uncommon that behavior is among dolphins. We agreed that it worked.

On this next page, I chose to use the chronological structure to tell the story of the Katrina dolphins, whose aquarium was destroyed by the hurricane and were washed out to sea. These dolphins stuck together, one female even producing milk for a baby dolphin, and were overjoyed when their trainers were able to rescue them. I felt that this interaction between dolphins and humans was best conveyed as a story. It seemed to teach about this moment, and pull more at the reader's heartstrings as a story rather than any of the other structures.

After modeling my process, writers then tried it out themselves. The chart on page 187 acted as a menu of choices for writers. We added to it and revised it as we worked, customizing the "how" and "when" as writers discovered more about each structure as they planned with them. My wish is for you to do the same, with the chart on the next page and any other chart I share—that you personalize it for your writers.

My Process to Choose a Structure

1. Zoom in on one topic within my writing

2. Think about what I want the reader to learn or know about this topic

3. Plan out a few different structures (just quick plans, not lots of writing)

4. Read over the plans and choose the one that best fits with what I want the reader to know or learn about the topic

Structure

One big thing that effected me was strucrure. I liked having the choice, so my writing can be what I wanted it to be. For example: when I wrote about black holes, it was hard to to problem and solution. However, there was many other choices I could've done. Cause and Effect suited me better. The freedom to have choice makes my writing less forced.

Choices for Structure in Informational Writing

Structure	How to Use It	When to Use It
Description	Introduce the topic/idea and further explain with facts and other information.	When you want to give an overview When you want to introduce a new topic or idea When you need to share an important collection of information
Cause and effect	Start with a cause, maybe as your topic sentence, and then follow with sentences and graphics that show the effect.	When you want to show how one thing impacts another When you want to show how something improved or worsened When you want to show the outcomes of certain events
Problem/ solution	Make the problem or misunderstanding clear right off the bat. Then share a variety of solutions or give great detail, maybe in a step-by-step, to one big solution.	When you want to show how something could possibly be solved When you want to correct misunderstandings with facts When you want to show how a challenge was resolved
Compare and contrast	Pick two topics or ideas that you want to compare. Keep the topics near each other so the reader can look back and forth. This might be on one page from paragraph to paragraph or two pages next to each other.	When you want to share the similarities and differences of a topic or idea When it is hard to describe without sharing something very different When you want to show the "before and after"
Chronological	You may want to number the steps, use a timeline, or write this as a story.	When you want to share events as they happened When you want to show how to do something When you want to tell the story about something rather than give only facts on it

We can also offer alternative structures within the essay format, especially for opinion and argument writing. These may still turn out to be five (or more) paragraphs, but the writer chooses the way the paragraphs unfold. Aimee Carroll-Matos, a seventh-grade teacher, offered two structures when writing a literary essay: the point-by-point structure and the block structure. When students planned their essay, they tried out both structures (and added or subtracted paragraphs as necessary) and chose the one that fit their overall argument the best. Aimee's tools follow. Note the detail she includes to help plan, yet simultaneously offering choice, so writers can choose the structure that works best for them.

ARGUMENTATIVE ESSAY for LITERARY ANALYSIS

"POINT by POINT" STRUCTURE

Introduction	**Paragraph 1: Introduction** • Hook • CLAIM (stay focused on question asked) • State 3 points
Body 1 Both Texts	**Paragraph 2: Focuses on POINT 1** • Topic sentence for BOTH texts • Detail sentence (paraphrased/1 text evidence) o Link back to CLAIM • Closing sentence
Body 2 Both Texts	**Paragraph 2: Focuses on POINT 2** • Topic sentence for both texts • Detail sentences of (paraphrased/1 text evidence) o Link back to CLAIM • Closing sentence
Body 3 Both Texts	**Paragraph 4: Focuses on POINT 3** • Topic sentences for both texts • Detail sentences of (paraphrased/1 text evidence) o Link back to CLAIM • Closing sentence
Conclusion	**Paragraph 4: Conclusion** • Restate claim • Restate topics • New thinking o Relate to the world

** Add a Counter Claim in the beginning of the Body Paragraphs **

"POINT by POINT" PREP-PLANNING

INTRODUCTION/**CLAIM**	
Focus 1:	Details:
Focus 2:	Details:
Focus 3:	Details:
CONCLUSION:	

ARGUMENTATIVE ESSAY for LITERARY ANALYSIS

"BLOCK" STRUCTURE

Introduction	Paragraph 1: Introduction to Topic • Hook • CLAIM (stay focused on question asked) • State general sentence of body paragraphs
Body 1	Paragraph 2: Text 1 • Topic sentence • Detail sentences of (paraphrased/1 text evidence) ○ Link back to CLAIM • Closing sentence
Body 2	Paragraph 3: Text 2 • Topic sentence • Detail sentences of (paraphrased/1 text evidence) ○ Link back to CLAIM • Closing sentence
Body 3	Paragraph 4: Similarities and Differences in BOTH Texts • Topic sentence • Detail sentences of (paraphrased/1 text evidence) ○ Link back to CLAIM • Closing sentence
Conclusion	Paragraph 4: Conclusion • Restate claim • Restate topics • New thinking ○ Relate to the world

** Add a Counter Claim in the beginning of one of the Similarities and Differences paragraphs **

"BLOCK" PRE-PLANNING

INTRODUCTION/**CLAIM**

TEXT 1:	TEXT 2:
Details:	Details:
Details:	Details:
Details:	Details:
Details:	Details:

Similarities and Differences:
•
•
•

CONCLUSION:

Aimee also shared her thoughts on offering choice in structure:

> I realized that even though I am the teacher, sometimes the student can have the most insight into his or her writing. Instead of fighting with them I have allowed them a choice, and given them a voice. Once I started allowing them to choose between two points of view, or determine the structure that they want to use, the writing immediately became theirs. Surprisingly,

my strongest students struggled most with the idea of choice. They wanted to make sure that it was "right." The fact that they were so uncomfortable with the idea of choice worried me, and motivated me even more to allow choice as often as possible. As a teacher stepping back and mentoring my students, rather than directing their writing, allowed them to achieve beyond my expectations. Their work was theirs.

Structure can also carry options in stories. Kurt Vonnegut, back in 1947, coined the "Universal Shapes of Stories." I have adapted four of them here, more geared toward Grades 3 through 8. Depending on your grade level and writers' levels of sophistication, a few or all of these structures may be shared as options. Perhaps your story writers can try out a few of these in quick plans before committing to one in a draft.

Four Shapes of Stories: Kurt Vonnegut

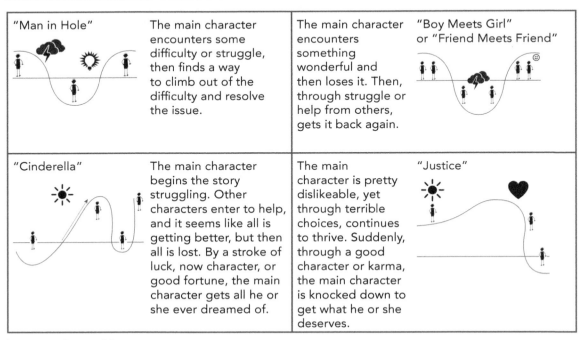

| "Man in Hole" | The main character encounters some difficulty or struggle, then finds a way to climb out of the difficulty and resolve the issue. | The main character encounters something wonderful and then loses it. Then, through struggle or help from others, gets it back again. | "Boy Meets Girl" or "Friend Meets Friend" |
| "Cinderella" | The main character begins the story struggling. Other characters enter to help, and it seems like all is getting better, but then all is lost. By a stroke of luck, now character, or good fortune, the main character gets all he or she ever dreamed of. | The main character is pretty dislikeable, yet through terrible choices, continues to thrive. Suddenly, through a good character or karma, the main character is knocked down to get what he or she deserves. | "Justice" |

Images source: Courtesy of clipart.com

In this section are a few ways of offering choice in structure as a form of feedback, but the options are vast, far beyond what was shared here. My hope is that these suggestions inspire you to create opportunities for choice in structure above and beyond these resources. The more you tinker with choice and structure with your own students in mind, the more you will support their ownership and agency.

Feedback That Offers Choices in Elaboration

Back when I first started teaching, I learned of an elaboration technique of "using sensory images." I loved this technique and taught it with gusto. In fact, I was very specific about those sensory images, teaching my writers to use all five senses. I then went one step further and actually required that all writers include sensory images in their writing. And even more, I required that they have a sensory image for each of the five senses somewhere in their writing. This was more important to me than actually having the writers choose where and when sensory images fit best. I was pretty much forcing the use of an elaboration technique. I still clearly remember the conversation I had with Marcus when I was urging him to use all of his senses so he could improve his grade. "Mrs. McGee," he pleaded. "There really was not a time in this whole story that I tasted *anything*." Remembering this makes me cringe—what was I thinking? I know I had the best intentions, my heart has always been in my teaching, but that was pretty terrible. If I could rewind back to that time over 20 years ago, I would do a few things differently. First, I would find a number of elaboration techniques to love, not just one. I would offer them as possibilities and model them in my own writing and create a menu of sorts from which my students could choose. And I would apologize to Marcus, and the others in my class, for stealing their ownership and agency.

In this section, I have created some sample charts that I wish I had back then in order to build elaboration choices into my feedback. These charts are meant to be for you, the teacher, to refer to in order to offer choices as purposeful, intentional, and writerly feedback. These charts are only scratching the surface and can and should be added to your ideas and techniques for your writers. I have also included some tips on using these choice charts to make them most useful for your writers.

Tips on Using the Elaboration Choice Charts

1. Add other techniques and choices. Personalize the chart. You can do this by writing a bit of that text type yourself and noticing the techniques you use. You will have both a technique added and a piece of writing with which to model.

2. Many of these techniques will need to be pretaught, studied in a mentor text, modeled, or otherwise made familiar to the writer before making them a choice.

3. The techniques listed may be too simple for some writers and too sophisticated for others. Be picky.

4. Two to four choices are usually sufficient when giving feedback. Too many choices can become overwhelming for the writer.

5. Elaboration does not always work out as planned. It is helpful to have someone to listen and give feedback on the elaboration choices. Use the peer feedback protocols from Chapter 5 for writers to get and give feedback on elaboration choices.

Pam, in offering choice in elaboration, sometimes displays these choices on colorful and writer-focused charts; see page 196 for an example. Notice the handwriting—both Pam and her writers created this collection of options.

Elaboration choices can create a sense of ownership and agency, and can make the writing sound delightfully sophisticated and voice-filled. When writers try out elaboration techniques, choose to keep them or revise them, and rework details within their chosen structure, true agency and ownership flourish. The tipping point of ownership and agency is when we give our students choice in grammar.

Choices for Elaborating in Narrative Writing

When the writer wants ...	Your feedback might include ...
The main character to come alive to the reader	Making them talk by using dialogue Sharing their inner thinking Describing small gestures or facial expressions Having another character react to the main character Including a memory (i.e., flashback) Making them struggle with a problem; showing that struggle in their thoughts and words
The setting to be crystal-clear	Describing the setting throughout the story, especially when the setting changes Including what the characters hear, smell, and see Having your character react to the setting ("what a lovely day at the beach," she thought) Including the setting in the character's actions ("she pushed her toes into the sand")
The bigger lesson or theme to emerge	Having the character act out of character and learn something big Having the character say out loud or to themselves what he or she learned Being the omniscient narrator, describing the lessons that were learned Having one character teach another character in their words and actions Using a symbol to reflect the learning, like the clouds parting and sun shining through

Available for download at **http://resources.corwin.com/McGee-Feedback**

Choices for Elaborating in Informational Writing

When the writer wants to ...	Your feedback might include ...
Explain a fact or collection of facts	Adding your thoughts about those facts
	Comparing those facts to something else ("a dolphin pod is like a family")
	Quoting directly from a source that explains the fact
	Rephrasing the fact to clarify ("In other words . . .")
	Adding a graphic that illustrates the fact(s), like a photo, diagram, chart, etc.
	Using an anecdote about that fact
Define content-specific words	Adding a definition inside parentheses
	Adding a definition inside commas, as an appositive
	Writing the definition in the next sentence
	Adding a graphic that illustrates and clarifies the definition
	Adding a textbox or sidebar with the definition
	Defining the words in a glossary
Create cohesion	Using transition words from paragraph to paragraph and sometimes sentence to sentence
	Designing subheadings that have similar patterns or wording
	In paragraphs, having your opening sentence and closing sentence say similar things
	Ensuring that all writing under a heading belongs there

 Available for download at **http://resources.corwin.com/McGee-Feedback**

Choices for Elaborating in Opinion/Argument Writing

When the writer wants to . . .	Your feedback might include . . .
Be even more convincing	Quoting from a reliable outside source Paraphrasing from reliable research Thinking of the reader and choosing words that are most convincing to that reader Explaining how the facts you choose to include support your overall point of view Studying the verbs and adjectives in your sentences and considering whether you should replace them with bolder words
Acknowledge the other side to strengthen your stance (counterclaim)	Disproving a myth that is considered a fact about the other side Naming the other side's position and then explaining why your position is better/stronger/the one with which to side Naming the other side's belief and explaining why they should not hold that belief Naming the other side's position and explaining why that position is incorrect, false, or otherwise mistaken
Wrap up your opinion/argument	Writing a few sentences that suggest next steps for the reader—a call to action Summarizing your major reasons and your point of view Highlighting one or two most significant pieces of evidence that support your stance Telling a quick story that illustrates a time or outcome when people sided with your argument Imagining what could happen if the readers agreed with your side and writing a few sentences to help the reader picture this too

 Available for download at **http://resources.corwin.com/McGee-Feedback**

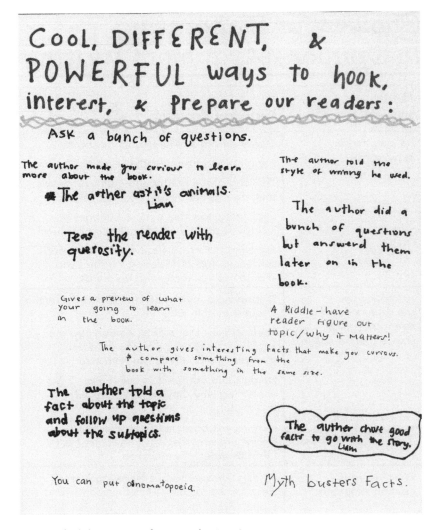

You can feel the energy of engaged writers!

 ## Feedback That Offers Choices in Grammar and Conventions

Grammar and conventions—the language of language, the rules English follows, and the polish on strong writing—is a hot-button topic in the world of education. Many debate the approaches to teaching grammar, yet none can deny the influence grammar can have when used wisely. Grammar has power. The misuse of grammar

weakens writing. Grammar and writing are not separate from each other. In fact, it is time to consider grammar as a tool and choice used to craft writing in meaningful, intentional ways. It's not grammar *and* style, like we thought it was—it's grammar *is* style.

Traditionally, though, grammar is taught through a workbook/worksheet focus—identifying, highlighting, labeling, rewriting, correcting—and is often separate from writing. Sometimes it feels as though grammar is a separate subject from writing altogether, or must be learned first before any writing is done. Research disproves these traditional approaches. As long ago as 1963, Braddock, Lloyd-Jones, and Schoer found "the teaching of formal grammar has a negligible or, because it usually displaces some instruction and practice in actual composition, even a harmful effect on the improvement of writing" (pp. 37–38). In 1986, George Hillocks, professor of education and English at the University of Chicago, shared his meta-analysis results on grammar instruction: "None of the studies reviewed for the present report provides any support for teaching grammar as a means of improving composition skills. If schools insist upon teaching the identification of parts of speech, the parsing or diagraming of sentences, or other concepts of traditional grammar (as many still do), they cannot defend it as a means of improving the quality of writing" (p. 172). George Hillocks again, this time with Michael Smith (1991), author of the grammar teaching book *Getting It Right,* shared: "Research over a period of nearly 90 years has consistently shown that the teaching of school grammar has little or no effect on students" (pp. 591–603). The research suggests what many of you are probably thinking, anyway—students need support in grammar, but the old ways of teaching grammar are not working.

What *does* work, then, in grammar instruction? Teaching grammar in the context of writing (Calkins, 1980; DiStefano & Killion, 1984; Ehrenworth & Vinton, 2005; Harris, 1962; Hillocks & Smith, 1991; Weaver, 1996). In other words, writers learn to punctuate by punctuating their writing. They learn to use sentence structure by crafting their own sentences. They learn writing with agreement by ensuring their words agree.

Writers want more than just learning grammar for grammar's sake, though. They want (whether they realize this or not) to harness grammar to make it work for their writing, with ownership and agency. When grammar is seen as a powerful crafting tool, writers develop those skills as part of their writing identity. Imagine writers who say, "I am the type of writer who crafts my sentences carefully, using and breaking the grammar rules for effect." It is possible! Especially when we offer choice in grammar.

Before diving into the sorts of choices we can offer as feedback in grammar, I want to clarify that I am not suggesting that writers ignore the rules of English. I am suggesting the opposite: that they learn the rules by using and choosing which rules to employ for their larger intention or meaning. For example, sentences need punctuation. This is a grammar rule. The choice lies in which type of punctuation to use for effect. Another rule is that we add quotes around dialogue. It is the writer's choice, though, where and how to tag the dialogue.

When we offer choice, we also keep from slipping into old feedback habits. Remember the "red-pen" thinking we explored in Chapter 1? Grammar and conventions is the area of feedback where the red pen starts to rear its ugly head. After all, that is how many of us were taught grammar. But, if we switch our focus from correcting to offering choices, we support ownership and agency in grammar usage. One way to keep focused on choice is to use the chart on the next page.

Grammar and Choice Feedback Chart

Grammar Skill	Questions You Might Pose (Research)	Choices
Punctuation	"What were you hoping your reader was thinking/feeling in this part?" "When did you want the reader to pause? Slow down? Stop? Read it like that out loud for me."	Use a semicolon (;) when two sentences are closely related and you don't want to use a conjunction. Use exclamation points sparingly. Too much excitement ends up making nothing feel exciting. Vary your periods and exclamation points for the right effect. The ellipse shows something exciting is about to happen . . . When reworking sentences, you may want to try out some different comma rules: • around an appositive (inserted bonus information midsentence) • when combining two simple sentences into a complex sentence • after a transitional word or phrase • in a trio of adjectives, using a comma between them
Sentence structure	"Let's revisit your goals and study your sentence structure to see if it is supporting your goals." "Have you considered the sentence types you are using?" "What are you hoping the reader thinks/feels/learns here? Do your sentences fit that goal?"	Simple sentences can be very effective for: • grabbing a reader's attention • summing up an argument • stating something simply and clearly • creating balance if the rest of your sentences are too long and lengthy Compound sentences are effective when: • you are looking to create a sense of balance or contrast between two (or more) equally important pieces of information • you have used lots of simple sentences and it is time to mix them up a bit • you want to show how two ideas are connected or related A complex sentence is most effective when: • you want to create the effect of long, flowing, wordy language • you want to end a sentence with your idea and build your idea into the first part of the sentence • it takes many words to express your ideas precisely
Verb tense and voice	"Let's consider the verb tense you have chosen. Does it meet with your goals?" "Let's make sure the verbs are fitting your overall purpose."	Use the present tense to make the reader feel like they are going through the moment with you. Use the past tense to help the reader feel a bit reflective on what has already happened. Use the future tense to help the reader imagine what will or can happen. Use the active voice most of the time. Choose the passive voice when you want to be vague about the subject of the sentence ("Issues arose").

Available for download at **http://resources.corwin.com/McGee-Feedback**

Tips for Using the Grammar and Choice Feedback Chart

1. Before offering choices, find out what effect or impact the writer was hoping to have in particular parts of his writing. It will help you choose what grammar will best make that impact. The "research" questions will help.

2. You might need to model grammar usage for writers. Showing how to make a grammar choice enables the writer to do this with more independence in the future.

3. Create small groups or writing clubs that study one type of grammar and those choices. They will become more solid in making those choices when working on it with others.

4. Revise, personalize, and modify so this chart fits your writers and your grade level.

5. When offering choices, start with one or two possibilities. Pick and choose—there are too many options here. For example, the many choices a writer can make around commas is too detailed a topic for one feedback conversation or lesson.

Following is an example of how one writer, named Jeanie, used choice to revise her sentence structure. (Jeanie was writing directly into a Google doc; that is why it is not a handwritten example.) When I met with her, she felt her sentence structure could use some revision 🎯 because pretty much every sentence was built the same and her piece didn't have that "pizazz" she felt the introduction ought to have. I shared three different ways of revising sentences, 🏯 which she typed right into her document. I modeled these by taking three sentences and revising them using all three choices (see bare bones writing in Chapter 4). The first paragraph is the one she originally wrote. The second is a revision using some sentence structure choices.

Sentence structure choices:

appositive

switch around one part and put it at the beginning with a comma

add onto the end of a sentence to explain more

Marian Anderson

Marian Anderson was an American contralto singer. She was a very important part in why African American people felt like they could become singers. She had an effect because of what happened to her and after she died what people thought about it. Her life and the events made her who she was and caused a movement. Her voice made a change.

Marian Anderson, an American contralto singer, is a very important part in why African American people felt like they could become singers. Before and after she died, she had an effect because of what happened to her and what people thought about it. Her life events made her who she was and caused a movement, which is why she was important to the history of singers. Her voice made a change.

While Jeanie could still spend a little more time working through her sentence structure choices, there is a big difference between the sophistication of the first attempt and the revision. All of that revision was done independently, without my coaching. More important, Jeanie remarked that she felt she took charge of her writing and was able to think about grammar—at least, sentence structure—differently now.

All in all, offering choice in grammar whenever possible creates a new dynamic around grammar instruction. Perhaps the term *grammar instruction* does not quite fit—instead, it is teaching style through grammar choices. When writers harness the power of grammar to craft and revise their writing, grammar is not only learned, it is used.

Techy Choice Making

My favorite way of blending choice and technology is in the way writers choose to publish their writing. Technology can bring an authentic audience to writing pieces or allow a writer to use a completely new medium. While I am sure there will be many new possibilities for publishing in techy ways, and technology is evolving at warp speed, here are a few that I have seen writers use. Many of these come from my favorite educational technology blog, Free Tech for Teachers, at www.freetech4teachers.com.

Google Docs and Google Classroom: This ever-evolving web-based alternative to Microsoft Office has taken classrooms to a new level of technology use. The possibilities seem to grow every day. I am a Google Drive convert—I wrote this entire book on Google Drive.

Podcasts: Podcasts are taking on a life of their own almost as an alternative to radio. Our students are following podcasts like they would a television series. Podcasts are also a fantastic medium for writers to read their writing and share with others. A podcast can be created on Voice Memo on an iPad, GarageBand on Mac, or SoundCloud online. You can find countless more options simply by searching the Internet.

Blogs: Blogs are a staple in my daily reading. Your writers can put their voice out into the world (or keep it just in the classroom or school) by setting up a space to blog. Google Classroom is great for this. I also like Kidblog, Edublog, and Blogger.

Wrapping It Up

We began this chapter thinking about our most disengaged, apathetic writers and the role choice can play in building ownership and agency. These are the writers who keep us up at night, the ones we struggle to reach. Choice will begin to make that struggle a little bit easier. Choice, though, is not only meant to empower our reluctant writers; it is meant to support all writers in creating investment and passion about writing. Choice is not limited to just one part of the writing process; it can be offered as feedback wherever writers are and whatever the writing program. As Luke, a seventh grader, shared, "If we never had a choice, the only thing I'd be interested about in school is recess." Choice is an integral part of risk taking and goal setting. It also holds a strong connection to our next feedback focus: when writers need learning to stick—feedback for reflecting.

Chapter 7

Feedback Comes Full Circle

Reflecting for Learning

We do not learn from experience . . . we learn from reflecting on experience.

—John Dewey

It was one of those moments all teachers hope for. It was mid-March. Rob Karklin and I stood off to the side of his classroom watching it all unfold. His seventh graders, knee-deep in researching topics for a feature article due the following week, were comparing resources with an eye for bias, considering the resource's publication date for validity, jotting down notes in self-chosen structures, and debating with one another on perspectives to take when writing their article. All *without* teacher support. It seemed all teaching and learning stars aligned: students deeply engaged in their work, learning from and with one another, unaware of us. We knew it was a moment to savor and also study. What, we asked ourselves, made this happen? What had made all of those lessons Rob taught on bias and validity, note-taking, and conversation stick? These moments are few and far between, and if we were to replicate it in future classes of students, we needed to examine the habitat in which these students writers thrived.

Rob is the kind of teacher who does many things to help learning stick, but for starters I asked him the lofty inquiry question, "What the heck did you do, and how can we bottle this?"

He smiled and said, "It is the students. They are amazing."

I told Rob that of all the sophisticated thinking and strategies for researching I heard, what was most amazing of all—and the elixir I wanted to bottle—was his students' agency. Independence. He and I could have taken the rest of the day off and those students would thrive. *They didn't need us.* Later, I sat down with Rob and asked many other questions, listening for what might have been the most relevant practice that accounted for his students' success. Among many other moves, Rob supports choice, creates a safe place for risk taking, models vulnerability, and works to support engagement at all costs—all practices I describe in this book. But the practice that came up most often in Rob's language as he described his teaching was this: reflection. He builds in moments of reflection. Each day, his students reflect on both their plans for writing and their writing progress. He has partners or small groups talk at least twice a day. A few times per week, he has students jot down their reflections. He often asks questions like, What was really hard? Can we figure out why it was such a bear? And he meets face to face with his students to have them reflect on their work. Reflection is a pivotal cog in the cycle of learning, and what Katie Charner-Laird (2003) calls "the mind's strongest glue."

Reflection solidifies student learning and lays the foundation for future learning. Reflection is the final piece of the puzzle in a feedback-rich classroom. Reflection as feedback comes in many shapes: The teacher can be reflecting on what she or he sees feedback from the teacher to support self-reflection, peer-to-peer reflection, reflection on writing and on the writer, and more. So far

> # Signs Learning Has Stuck
>
> - Writers are employing a variety of strategies
>
> - Writers show ownership and agency by making informed choices
>
> - Writers ask for specific feedback and help that quickly moves them into more independent work
>
> - Writers teach others about strategies they have used
>
> - Writers give feedback to others in careful, thoughtful ways
>
> - Writers move smoothly from one part of writing to the next (e.g., drafting to revision)

in this book we have explored the many varied ways teachers and students can provide feedback to one another. To come full circle in our tour of feedback that moves writers forward, in this chapter we look at how to teach our writers to give feedback to themselves. We explore the many reasons why we ought to build in moments of reflection and the many ways we can support our students in reflecting for learning.

Reflecting for Learning

Reflecting is providing feedback for yourself.

I often post this statement on the classroom wall for students to consider. And even though I sometimes get eye rolls when I quote John Dewey (who students may think is as old as our founding fathers), I do it anyway: "We don't learn from experience . . . we learn from reflecting on experience." Students need to understand as much as we do that when we examine what we've done, it helps us own the best parts, jettison what didn't work so well, and apply our learning from one context to the next.

Reflection may well be one of the most overlooked tools in our teaching toolbox. In the hustle and bustle of time-crunched classrooms it must be the intentional choice of the teacher to build in moments of reflection or it can easily be one of the last and least common approaches to helping learning stick.

Reflecting is something we all do in life, so it only makes sense that we make it a part of the school learning context. For example, it is culturally expected that we end each calendar year with reflections and resolutions. Journals and even leather-bound notebooks line the shelves of stores each year, so that's got to mean something about our propensity for jotting down reflections. Speaking personally, I reflect after moments of challenge and sadness, and after moments of joy, and though I don't consciously do it with a learning benefit in mind, the process does help me learn. In a moment of challenge, writing helps me figure out how I can incorporate it so it adds meaning to my life and not just hardship. With moments of happiness, I write to internalize those moments so they become a part of me. When we lose someone famous or dear to us, we often reflect in eulogies and obituaries on their well-lived life so we can keep a piece of them with us. In the practice of yoga, there is a time of reflection—Shavasana—the pose that allows for the integration of the practice. There are spaces that compel reflection, especially those places of great emotion or significance: from the benches placed carefully in front of seminal art pieces in a museum to the reflection pools at the 9/11 Memorial. Reflection makes sure we do not forget, a defining condition of being human so that we understand the meaning of our experience (Mezirow, 1990).

Reflection is a practice backed by education researchers. When teachers carve out time for reflection in their classrooms they create the opportunity to "ensure that students are fully engaged in the process of making meaning . . . so that students are the producers, not just the consumers, of knowledge" (Costa & Kallick, 2008).

Reflection helps learning stick in a way that creates transfer (the use of learning at another place and time). Without reflection there is often a breakdown of transfer or a "failure to generalize learning from one situation or problem to another" (Johnston, 2004, p. 43). Harvard Business School in its working paper "Learning by Thinking: How Reflection Aids Performance" (Di Stefano et al., 2014) also studied the impact of reflection on learning. Not only did it find that "reflection is a powerful mechanism by which experience is translated into learning," it also concluded that "individuals perform significantly better on subsequent tasks when they think about what they learned from the task they completed."

Reflection as Feedback

Let's take a moment and imagine the inner dialogue that a struggling writer has running through his mind, often a soundtrack of negative statements: "I can't write. Everyone else can do this but I cannot. My spelling is terrible. I am not a writer." This writer is actually giving himself feedback—feedback that is unproductive, damaging, and debilitating. When we teach writers how to give themselves feedback that is productive, restorative, and empowering, we have given them the key to unlock the power of the writer within. Reflection is the opportunity to teach writers how to create, capture, and use their inner feedback.

We teachers are still an integral part of the reflection process by providing structures and time for feedback, even offering some or our own reflections to and about the writer. Likewise, reflection offers a way for writers to use themselves and their own learning to give personal feedback. For example, perhaps a writer takes a few moments to read over her writing and think, "What have I tried here that is working? What have I learned that I can use or try in the future?" The writer is designing her own feedback, personalized for herself and her writing, by contemplating next steps, ideas, moments of strength—the very same things the teacher or fellow students may offer as feedback. It is important not to underestimate the value of the feedback we offer ourselves—these thoughts shape our actions and can define our writing identity. With this in mind, let's start to unpack the important parts of reflection for writers.

Key Characteristics

Reflection that supports learning, transfer, and positive self-feedback has a few simple yet important characteristics. Let's take a look at one student's reflection and the characteristics that make this strong, useful, and "sticky." In this reflection, Laura Sarsten asked her fifth graders to take a moment to consider one of the questions they ask themselves when writing and to determine and describe the impact of that question.

Lana's Reflection!

Making decisions and choices to develop our persuasive writing pieces. How can we balance dense research based evidence with authentic rich thinking?

The question that helped me most was . . .

"Does this piece of thinking/Text Evidence (T.E.) relate to my claim?"

As a result I was able to . . .

In my writing I noticed that I used T.E. and thinking but it didn't really tie together, or make much sense. Asking myself this question helped in many ways. For instance as a result I was able to stay more on topic. I also thought that my thoughts and T.E. made more sense. In other words, this led me to have cohesion with my claim and my thoughts and T.E. supporting, not hurting. Last, this also helped to make sure that my stance stood out to the reader, with the T.E. almost shocking the reader and keeping them interested. Furthermore, using thoughtful T.E. and thinking that made sense and held integrity of writing and voice.

There are three attributes on this reflection form worth noting.

- **A reflection focus:** Laura did not just leave her writers to their own devices. She took an important instructional focus and made it a point of reflection. This broad concept or idea helps target the reflection in such a way that the writer has a direction without the task seeming restrictive. The concept of balancing "dense research based evidence with authentic rich thinking" was a major theme in the class's work across many days. In fact, students gave feedback to one another on this concept. Now it is time to give themselves some feedback. Choosing a focus helps the writer approach reflection with direction.

- **Structure and space:** This reflection form brings the writer through the process of reflection, with a kind of open-floor-plan architecture that guides students without herding their

thinking too much in a particular direction. Most important, ample space is provided for the student to think and to
write, so that there is room for the learner to make it personal,
authentic, and organic. Each of Laura's students' reflections
was unique—a sign that Laura hit the right balance of structure and space. A reflection tool should be both structured
and open.

- **A look at actions and outcomes:** It is one thing when a
  writer solely reflects on writerly actions taken—this is helpful in and of itself. Adding the next dimension of reflecting
  on the *outcomes* of those choices and actions makes learning even more "sticky." Look at the intricacy and breadth
  of Lana's outcomes—she writes of focus, cohesion, audience, clarity, and "integrity of writing and voice." While I
  am aware that not all writers, younger or older than Lana,
  will have such thoughtful, deep, and diverse reflections, a
  look at actions and outcomes still can stretch any writer to
  peer more closely at the impact of their choices. In turn, the
  consideration of outcomes prompts the writer to ask: Which
  actions do I want to be "portable?" What do I want to carry
  into future writing experiences?

Yes, reflection helps learning stick in important ways, helps rewrite
the inner dialogue of the struggling writer, and also creates other
constructive outcomes for your writers and their identities. Here
are a few:

- **Reflection creates risk takers:** One of the wonderful
  things I found when writers reflect on the risks they took is
  they are more apt to take risks in the future. Reflecting allows
  writers to think back and mull over the discomfort and vulnerability they may have felt when taking risks and then
  notice the outcomes of the risk taking—concluding at the
  very least "I survived the discomfort of taking a risk" and, we
  hope, "When I take risks, unexpected and astounding things
  happen in me and in my writing." Reflecting helps writers
  power through the hard parts of a next writing venture, as
  they can think, "Hey, I've been stuck before. I know what to
  do from here." One student writer's words say it all: "When

I reflect on the risks I took, I am proud of myself. I don't feel as nervous to make mistakes."

- **Reflection creates goal setters:** Reflection is often paired with planning next steps. It is a natural flow. For example, when I reflect on a lovely, restful, fun vacation, I instantly begin to imagine what I can do to plan for another. In the same vein, if I reflect on the cheesecake I baked that flopped, I think about what I will (or won't) do when I try my hand at baking again. It is the same with writing. When I reflect back on my own writing work, I either think about and plan how I will replicate what worked in my writing or what I will do to avoid what didn't. Those become either larger or smaller goals for me. The same happens with our writers. With moments of reflection, they take the time to think about what has worked, what has not, and what their next steps might be. One sixth grader, explaining his goal setting, shared: "When I am finished writing for the day I reflect and jot what I've done and make plans for next steps, making those my goals."

- **Reflection creates choice makers:** One of reflection's closest companions is ownership and agency. Reflection puts the writing squarely in the hands of the writer and says, "Where are we going from here? It's up to you!" When writers reflect not only on the choices they made, but the impact of those choices, they become more careful choice makers. Writers learn that choice making relies heavily on themselves, the writers, and their writing is a true representation of how much they contemplated their choices and made use of all they have learned and all they know. Reflection also helps the writers consider any choices they should have made. The act of reflecting on one's own writing requires the writers to own their processes and choices and supports their next steps such as requesting specific feedback, revising, restructuring, polishing, and rethinking their work.

- **Reflection creates happier writers:** Part of the science of happiness is a little brain chemical called dopamine— a neurotransmitter that, among a few jobs, controls the feeling of positivity. When dopamine is released, we feel good. The triggers for this release can range from a bite of a favorite food, to giggling at a puppy, to gaining the attention of someone we admire, to any other similar experiences. Another trigger for dopamine release is a sense of accomplishment. In other words, when we feel accomplished, we feel happy, and we want to feel that again. Reflection can help us seek out and find that sense of accomplishment. Sociologist Christine Carter writes in her book *The Sweet Spot* (2015) that "even something as small as a short mental victory dance can trigger a little hit of dopamine, enough to tell your brain to repeat whatever you just did" (p. 63). She suggests that we all congratulate ourselves for the smallest and biggest accomplishments with a moment of "Yay me!" Reflection helps us dig out those accomplishments from the complex ins and outs of writing and builds in the moments to say, "Yay me, I wrote though I felt frustrated!" or "Yay me, I took a few more steps toward my goal today!" or "Yay me, after lots of tries, I worked out the sentences in just the way I wanted them to flow!" These moments of tiny celebrations make for happier writers.

Reflection is the common thread among all of the writer-centered feedback 👓 I have written about across this book, pulling together the many concepts and experiences as important stepping-stones in learning the complex, challenging, awe-inspiring, creative experience that writing is. In the latter part of this chapter we will explore the many ways to use reflection when it's time for learning to stick, including both writer-centered and writing-centered reflections, and the gray area that connects both.

Reflection, in time-crunched classrooms, can often fall to the bottom of the instructional to-do list. On the next page are some ideas for making time for reflection.

It was extremely hard for me to select the reflection tools to share with you—the amazing teachers I worked with had over 100 to share with me. All of them, though, seemed to follow a particular process that you may want to follow as well when customizing time for reflection with your students.

Tips and Pointers to Build in Time for Reflection

- Take a few moments to reflect daily. At the end of a lesson or the end of the writing time, partake in a 3-minute reflection using some standard questions to guide writers into the reflection quickly.

- If you have students who come and go between classes, build in some reflection time during transitions. These can be part of the traditional "Do Now" or a standard part of how you start each day with a fun label like "Deliberate and Dream" or "Reflect and Envision" or whatever title you may find inspires your students.

- What we schedule shows what we value. Go ahead and schedule in when you want reflection. Put it on your calendar, in your plan book, or on the board. Anticipate the time as a community.

- Sometimes there are moments of waiting for an assembly or lunch or a visitor. Squeeze quick reflections into those small pockets of time.

- Make it part of your unit or planning as a consistent part of the learning process. Perhaps you have a natural flow to all units or topics—I like to build in reflection as we shift through the different stages of the writing process. Others like to build in reflection between writing pieces.

 # Creating for Your Students a Writer-Centered Reflection

1. Think of something you value about the work of a writer or within the writer's identity.

2. Make that the focus of the reflection.

3. Ask questions that help the writer look back on that focus, including actions and outcomes.

4. Put those questions into a structure that gives space for answers. Sometimes that space is in the margin of the writing, sometimes it is on sticky notes, sometimes it is on more formal tools.

Writer-Centered Reflecting

While all of the reflection tools I share in this chapter will support both the growth of the writing and the writer, I have divided the tools into those that lean more toward one side of the coin or the other simply to organize them all. You can pick and choose whichever reflections are timely and useful for your students. I have also tried to share the tools in a progression from the more simple to the more complex. If your writers are not familiar with reflecting, start with one of the first reflection tools. If they are more comfortable with introspective work, perhaps you would want to choose a tool shared a bit later on. I know that all of these tools, no matter the complexity or familiarity to your writers, will create moments of reflection to help learning stick.

 ## Quotation Reflection

Maybe reflecting on one's own writing is a little scary right off the bat. If that is the case, reflection might begin with some inspirational quotes. Pam Koutrakos offers her writers a chance to do this often. Classrooms all over display quotes to act as inspiration for writers. Pam takes this concept one step further and asks students to reflect on the quote. She likes to choose quotes that reflect a bigger concept, habit of mind, or inner quality she feels her students would benefit by contemplating. She asks writers to think about and jot down their interpretations of the quote.

> # Ways of Using Quotes for Reflection
>
> 1. Pick a quote that inspires you and your writers. Quotes that celebrate the qualities of a strong writing identity are especially helpful.
>
> 2. Ask your writers to think and jot on a sticky note their interpretation of the quote.
>
> 3. Talk about the reflections and interpretations as a group.

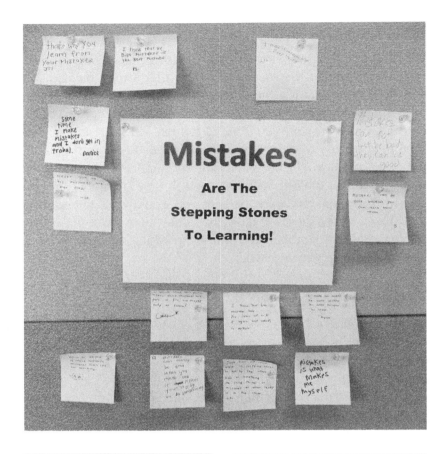

The uses of quotes to spark conversations are springboards for so much more, as Pam describes. They become mini-mantras to which we refer as we struggle, persevere, and celebrate learning both inside and outside the classroom.

Favorite Mistakes

Perhaps a little later on, maybe after a few days of writing or at the end of a writing piece, you might ask your students to reflect on their favorite mistake. This not only gives permission to make mistakes, but reminds students of the value of mistakes in learning. It creates a culture where mistakes are valued and perceived as moments of important learning. Here are a few reflections on mistakes from Laura's classroom.

My favorite mistake was when…

I wasn't taking time on my work and I wasn't caring about my work. This mistake was my favorite because, once I relized it I said "this isn't changing anything" and changed my behavior

---

My favorite mistake was when…

My Favorite mistake was on the first day of fifth grade, when I never pictured myself as a writer. Boy, was I wrong!

While this reflection sounds paradoxical, it acknowledges (even celebrates) the moments where a growth mindset and underwater mindframes fueled learning.

Favorite Mistakes Pointers

1. Celebrate mistakes by asking the question, "What was your favorite mistake?" Or by giving a sentence starter: "My favorite mistake was . . ."

2. Encourage writers to explain why and how that mistake helped them learn.

3. Talk about and celebrate these mistakes and consequential learning in small groups or the whole class.

    Underwater Mindframes Reflection

Remember, back in Chapter 4, when we explored the inner workings of a writer through Sylvia Duckworth's graphic? When writers not only expect these moments of underwater work but also reflect on them, the writer continues her path of inner growth. Without reflection, these underwater mindframes could go unnoticed. One student reflected on a few of these underwater skills and jotted down her thoughts.

Underwater Mindframes Reflection

1. Share the iceberg graphic and discuss the different words and what it all means. Maybe go back to Chapter 3 for wording on the comparison of the formation of glaciers, icebergs, and writing.

2. Ask writers to pick a few of these underwater mindframes that helped buoy their writing and jot about it.

3. Ask writers to reflect on the graphic itself and its implications on writing.

4. Share in conversation within groups or the whole class.

The Iceberg Illusion

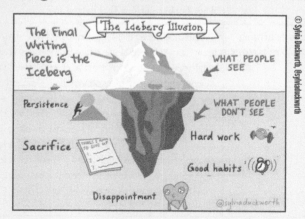

With all of her brilliance, Sylvia Duckworth created this Iceberg Illusion illustration. In the space below, discuss what you think the image represents and how it relates to your learning lives this trimester. Remember, success isn't just a "fluke"; it involves sacrifices, struggles, and loads of hard work!

This image can be represented to everyone's lives as a writer and a learner. Everyone who sees how successful you are and sometimes believes that you are just "lucky." However, I believe that there is something deep beneath the surface. It is what he/she goes through to get to what you see. This iceberg represents to my learning because I have noticed in our classroom that we judge others on the piece of writing that we read from them. For instance, we tend to say, "Wow that girl is really good at writing. It just comes easily to her, I guess." But what we don't know is all of that hard work it takes to get there. In addition, the image somewhat makes me think of a boat approaching the iceberg. It only sees the tip of it. To see the other part submerged, the boat must sink itself. Furthermore, without sinking you won't ever see the part of that incredible person that is hidden and most people don't consider.

In the space below discuss your experiences with some of the underwater skills. Remember to be open and honest; that's what reflection is all about.

Underwater Mindframe	What You Did and How That Helped You
Good habits: These are the "healthy" choices we make as writers and readers, like writing/reading every day, making the most of our time, setting goals.	Good habits. This is something that we don't always honestly respond to when we think about it. However, one thing that helps me a lot is setting healthy intentions on what I will accomplish that day.

(Continued)

(Continued)

Underwater Mindframe	What You Did and How That Helped You
Disappointment: In our learning lives sometimes things don't work out as planned.	Disappointment is a big part of my life as a learner. I have faced so many struggles in writing that almost make me give up, but for some reason I persevere. I faced this struggle by thinking why I started this; my spark of imagination before I began the writing project/ struggle. In addition, I found it also helpful to talk it out. This helped me by releasing my struggles and disappointment and using their advice. To add on, sometimes disappointment can be helpful towards reflecting and seeing, "what <u>could I have done</u> <u>differently? Better? Less of?</u>"

 Template available for download at **http://resources.corwin.com/McGee-Feedback**

Good Habits: These are the choices we make as writers that show we are making the most of our time.	Pick one habit you know will benefit you the most. Vow to do that every day. Good habits are not always fun but they can make you feel good in the end. Celebrate those good feelings.	A good habit I developed/strengthened in this unit was… writing strong and long when we were drafting. I will continue to do this because… it will make me strong learner and I will get more down.
Disappointment & "Failure:" In writing, sometimes things don't work out as planned.	Don't ignore disappointment- Learn from disappointment. Think, "How did I get here and how will I get out of here?" Think, this is disappointing now, but now forever. "Failure" is a gift! When things have not gone well, we learn. Jot and use what you will learn from this disappointment. "Failure" sometimes feels terrible but is like eating a really healthy, not very yummy vegetable. It helps us grow. Name the changes you plan on making because of this failure.	I felt disappointment when… when I tried on endings but none worked Instead of giving up, I … because … I did not give up I keep try in till I fond the right lead. What I learned from this was … don't give up at tuff times.

One teacher's modified reflection tool using the same concepts and personalizing it for her class.

Reflecting on Risk Taking

Taking risks can certainly have its rewards, and when writers have a moment to reflect on the risks they took, they are more apt to take risks again. When having the chance to really notice what happens when they do, and taking a moment to feel accomplished because of it, writers are happier and more willing to stretch and grow. Take a look below at the wise words from one third grader on the risks he took.

3. How does it feel to take a learning risk? Explain.

It felt uneasy at first, but when I started getting into rhythm it felt like I was accomplishing something great. I also felt like I was learning something important.

4. What can I do to encourage you to take MORE learning risks? How can I support you?

mrs. K is already encouraging me everyday to take new risks and accomplish more and become smarter.

If we want to develop into fearless, fruitful, independent writers, then we have to make it crystal-clear that we admire risk taking.

 ## Writing Identity Reflection

Back in Chapter 3, I shared a way of getting to know your writers with a writing identity survey. Since we know that writers' identity has a direct effect on their writing, it may be important to take a moment, both for your knowledge and the students' awareness, to reflect on the evolution of their writing identity across time. You may want to use that survey again as is, or ask students to consider writing a bit longer about particular aspects of the survey. Laura tried the latter with a few starters:

I am the type of writer who . . .

Something I notice about my writing is . . .

A risk or technique I want to try is . . .

How this will help me become a better writer is . . .

I am the kind of writer who . . .

Likes to write fiction because I can let my crazy imagination soar. I also like writing so I can get down my thoughts on something I want to write or anything. I can also write anywhere during a loud party or when no one's home.

Something I notice about my writing is . . .

It doesn't have that much punctuation besides periods and commas. In informal writing I mainly just put info and not thinking or ideas. I can expand on my writing in every topic even in math responses.

A technique I want to try is . . .

Adding suspense because I usually just shove things that are important in people's faces I don't make them think about it. This will help me because I can be a better writer and make people think hmm this guys a good writer.

I'm the kind of writer who . . .

I'm the writer who can elaborate thoughts and ideas. I also can include various thinking stems, transitions, and T.E. into my work/response. I can balance both the T.E. and my thoughts/ideas equally instead of having too much of them.

Something I notice I do as a writer is . . .

Something I notice I do is I will make it hard to have flow in my responses. I can sometimes will repeat certain ideas or T.E. I will confuse myself that quantity is more important than the quality of the work. Even though you should elaborate your thoughts, the quality of the work is more important.

A writing technique/risk I want to try is . . .

A writing technique I will like to try is to have more emotion and depth into my writing. Sometimes I would just state facts or some of my thoughts. But I would never but emotion into my non-fiction writing. I sometimes don't know when to include the emotion or how to solve this I will keep rereading my work to see when to include emotion.

How will this this help me become a better writer is . . .

By adding more emotion will help as a writer by putting more of my perspective into my writer. By just saying facts and some thoughts doesn't show my perspective about my topic, but if I add emotion it will show my perspective about my topic.

Steps for Writing Identity Reflection

1. Begin with a few questions or sentence stems to spark the writer's thinking.

2. Ask the writer to choose a few of the questions and stems to use to jot his or her reflection.

3. Encourage examples and anecdotes in his or her jots.

4. Celebrate by discussing and/or displaying these reflections.

 ## Symbolic Reflection

Perhaps an artsy reflection tool is what your writers respond to. If so, try out what Laura did with her writers. She asked them to paint or draw a picture that symbolized their learning journey that trimester. The writers needed to look within, at those important parts of their writing identity, and the many parts and pieces of learning and writing, creating a symbol for each of those parts. Laura then asked for a brief description of those symbols and how they relate to the writer's learning journey. Meghan, the writer in the example, symbolized some important essentials such as growth mindset, ownership, planning, reflection, and accomplishments. I adore this writer's sophisticated look at the learning process—just so insightful!

> My picture represents many things.
> For example, the road represents the never
> ending learning. The GPS represents planning
> for the future. The review mirror represents
> reflecting on your past accomplishments.
> Also, the steering wheel symbolizes taking
> your learning into your OWN hands. Don't
> forget, the flowers are ment to show your
> acomplishments and lastly, the sparkles
> on the car symbolizes my growth mindset
> this trimester. All in all, my picture represents
> the essentials in learning.

We know the writer's identity shapes the writing itself, so it is important for writers to have some introspective time, to note their changes and growth. It will also be useful for the writers to take a look at their writing to reflect on and solidify their learning.

Writing-Centered Reflections

As we begin to explore a variety of ways we can support writers and their reflections of their own writing, let's take a moment to clarify

Learning Journey Steps for Students

1. Think about your learning journey over the past few weeks. What have been the most important parts of that journey? Jot a few down.

2. Think of a symbol that best represents those parts that you jotted down. Sketch or describe.

3. Paint or draw a picture using those symbols.

4. Write an explanation of those symbols and how they contributed to your learning journey.

some essentials when reflecting on the writing itself. I feel strongly that reflection and grading should be separate experiences. If writers are expected to study their writing and writerly moves candidly and openly, they must be able to do so without the pressure of the grade. Knowing their reflection can influence their grade skews the reflection, making them either more critical or more generous with their self-feedback. If you must couple reflection and grades, please take a look back at Chapter 2 for ways to lessen the ill-effects of this pairing. Trust, though, that the act of reflection will help your writers grow and their writing will be that much stronger as well. To optimize the impact of reflection, keep grading out of sight and mind. The following tools, then, should be used for reflection in the absence of grading.

I have organized the collection of writing-centered reflection tools similarly to the organization of the writer-centered tools: from more simple to more complex. Again, choose the tool(s) according to your writers' comfort and experience with reflection and consider varying them throughout the year.

Teacher Reflection of the Writer: Feedback That Looks at Then and Now

To be reflective means "to mentally wander through where we have been and to try to make some sense out of it" (Costa & Kallick, 2008). When we take time to reflect as teachers on the work of our students, the results are abundant: We have a chance to name and celebrate students' learning so that they internalize and intentionally use new skills with purpose. As a mother, I am instinctively doing this all the time with my soccer goalie daughter—I will say, "I remember when you first learned what a soccer ball was. Now you're stopping soccer balls from passing the goal line with your fearless attack on the ball." Joy and pride, as well as a feeling of greater confidence, is evident in both her face and her next time on the field. We can be the same for our students. We have the outsider's perspective that the writer does not. This sort of reflection might sound like, "I remember when you were stuck coming up with ideas. Now you are full of lots of ideas, have written so many of them down, and have opened up a whole lot of possibilities for yourself." Pam shares this both in conversation and in writing, by jotting on sticky notes and leaving those notes with the writer. In her note on the next page, Pam realized what a huge leap this writer took—in the past there was a little reluctance in revising, particularly in trying out a few ways of writing sentences or structuring paragraphs to pick just the right one. Now, the writer has built a few possible closings, revising and revising again. Pam wanted to reflect on this process and celebrate it with a small note.

Tips for Writing "Then and Now" Reflections

1. Think about what the writer has struggled with in the past.

2. Name what the writer is doing now that is different, even in the slightest way.

3. Share the payoff this difference has had in the writing or for the writer.

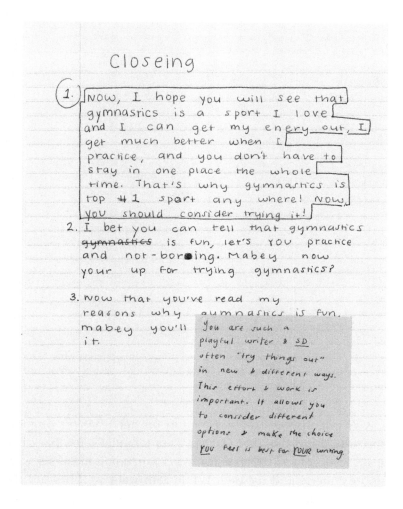

Closeing

(1.) Now, I hope you will see that gymnastics is a sport I love and I can get my enery out, I get much better when I practice, and you don't have to stay in one place the whole time. That's why gymnastics is top #1 sport any where! Now, you should consider trying it!

2. I bet you can tell that gymnastics ~~gymnastics~~ is fun, let's you practice and not-boraing. Mabey now your up for trying gymnastics?

3. Now that you've read my reasons why gumnastics is fun, mabey you'll it.

You are such a playful writer & SD often "try things out" in new & different ways. This effort & work is important. It allows you to consider different options & make the choice you feel is best for YOUR writing.

 ## Reflection on Feedback

One eighth grader's words from a few years back ring in my ears. When I asked what sort of feedback she had just gotten from her teacher she replied, "The same feedback I always get." Honestly, I cannot remember exactly what that feedback was on—paragraphing or punctuating or whatever—I just know that this writer was not learning from the feedback. I realize this happens all the time, and while reflection is not always the answer, it is one answer. When students not only hear feedback but take some time to reflect on that feedback, and anticipate that they will have to, there is an increased likelihood that the writer will learn from the feedback.

Reflection: I feel like when I plan out my writing, and stay more organized with my writing, I end up writing exactly what I want to say, but in fewer sentences. when I think ahead about my writing, don't end up going on and on and on about minor details that aren't important to my story. I havent completely met my goal yet, but, for example, when I was writing my star wars persuasive essay the other day, I was very planned out and I knew what I was going to write, so I was able to write exactly what I wanted to say in just a few sentances in each paragraph writing shorter sure helps me stay more organized and finish a LOT faster!

This student's reflection shows he's learned through experience what Mark Twain expressed in his famous line, "Sorry, I didn't have time to write a short letter, so I wrote a long one instead."

This is an example of Sam's reflection on her teacher's ongoing feedback. In a nutshell, her teacher, Lesa Jezequel's, feedback had been suggestions and strategies on ways Sam could make her writing more concise and focused. While Sam went well beyond the allotted space for reflection (the irony is not lost on me!), she did so with precise details relevant to her focus. This illustrates that Sam not only took Lesa's advice to heart but also has been working at it with some specific strategies. Notice, also, how simple this reflection is. There are no questions, no prompts, no stems. It simply has a space marked for reflection. Reflection can be as brilliantly simple as that!

 ## Reflection as Celebration

When we think about reflecting on one's own writing, it can be surprisingly helpful to have someone else reflect on the writing first and offer their feedback. Sometimes, when a writer is deeply invested in his writing, it is hard to see what is really working and what needs work. I know that having others take a look and offer some suggestions on my writing is an integral part of my process—this book would not be what it is without my editors Wendy Murray and Rosanne Kurstedt, who are able to offer their feedback. They have found and named words, sentences, sections, and chapters that are strong and effective while also pointing out places for more revision, clarification, and cohesion. Their reflections help refresh my writer's eye. I see my writing differently and approach future writing that much more aware and equipped.

We can take this same concept into the classroom. Before asking writers to reflect on their writing, ask someone else to try it first. The reflections of others can guide their personal reflections. This needs to be approached carefully, though. Unlike my relationship with Wendy and Rosanne, students don't always trust that their fellow writers have their best intentions in mind. In other words, there is a whole tangled web of social challenges our writers are often working through, and it can be intensely uncomfortable to share their writing with someone they don't entirely trust. That's why, beginning with reflection that takes on a tone of celebration, we can create a community where writers are openly sharing feedback/reflections with one another.

In my opinion, the world of education needs more celebrations, and I find inspiration to build in more celebrations in the words of Byrd Baylor: "Last year I gave myself one hundred and eight celebrations—besides the ones they close school for" (1986). And, while we can, of course, pull out all of the stops for a writing celebration, a reflection as celebration does not need too much planning. Celebration, as Katherine Bomer says, does not have to be a marching band and party favors. It is honoring, marking, or making something public. I am suggesting that reflections have a celebratory tone, more than a party atmosphere.

And with that tone, writers can offer other writers their reflections. They can jot them down on sticky notes or write them using the comments of a digital document; they can be written by many on one piece of paper or typed onto a spreadsheet. As long as the comments celebrate the important work of the writer.

I liked how You started
Your intro with a
strong statement.
I also liked how you
talked about how the
Indians were their for
thousands of years! I
totally agree with
you.

-Very cohesive headings
-Intertwining message
- Nice Intro
-Very emotional
  ending

Feedback that moves writers forward, plain and simple

Tips for Writers Celebrating Other Writers' Work

1. Think of all you know about this type of writing and this particular writer.

2. Name what is working in quick statements. This can be a part, a sentence, a word, or the entire piece. Be specific.

3. Jot it down and give it to the writer to reflect on your words. So, in essence, one writer is offering feedback for the other to consider.

Before-and-After Reflections

When there is a reluctance to revise (and there often seems to be!), reflection can be a handy tool. Laura's writers took a little time to share how they revised at the sentence level. This reflection was posted—another form of celebration—to show others the power of revision. Laura simply asked students to divide the page into two columns, showing a before (what my writing used to say . . .) and after (what my writing says now . . .).

What my writing used to say...	What my writing says now...
"The Maya were a group of civilized people that was known for their high-level knowledge."	"The Mayan culture were a refined group of geniuses and were well-respected for revolutionizing mankind and the way we live."
"This was one of the first pieces of evidence of early numbering."	"This chart of numbers 0-19 shaped in patterns is one of the earliest discoveries of the origin of numbering."
"How did El Castillo play a role in the Mayans lifestyle and beliefs?"	"How does the Mayan adjust and learn from El Castillo? In addition how does this impact their lifestyles and beliefs?"

Before-and-after reflection

Before-and-After Reflections: A Few Tips

- Often, reflection comes after something is relatively complete. This reflection can be used across a few days within the revision process. Meaning, when a student revises a sentence, he can make it part of the reflection and head back into writing. This approach is a strong encouragement to revise, especially for those who are reluctant to revise.

- Build in some partnership time to talk through the before and after. Sometimes the partner can suggest one more revision to the sentence. The first revision is not always the end of the revision process.

- Have some model or mentor sentences for students to study to help with the revision process.

- Before-and-after reflections are not limited to sentences. You may want writers to reflect and celebrate the before and after of paragraphs, chunks of writing, titles, etc.

 ## Line-by-Line Reflection Into Revision

Sometimes our writers need a deep, detailed reflection experience, and we may want that experience to span more than just a skill or two. If so, you may want to use this line-by-line reflection from Pam. Before writing is considered completed, Pam often asks her students to reflect on the many writing choices they made and the variety of writing skills they learned by engaging in a deep, detailed reflection.

Pam carves out a solid chunk of time and creates a tool that supports writers in that intricate, reflective experience. She starts by listing skills and strategies for writers to study in their writing, asking them to read line by line, in search of those skills. For example, if she taught using transitional language, Pam added it to the list and her

PART 1: ANNOTATING OUR OWN WORK

1. Find your lead. Underline your lead in red.
2. Put a red star next to your OPENING/INTO paragraph.
3. Put a blue star next to your first BODY paragraph.
4. Put a green star next to your second BODY paragraph.
5. Put a yellow star next to your THIRD body paragraph.
6. Underline each transition word you used (throughout your essay) in orange.
7. Underline your "strong closing statement(s)" in purple.

Questions to think about/check on:

How many different pieces of evidence did you have in each body paragraph?

Did you use a combination of lists, mini-stories, and "other" evidence as proof?

PART 2: REFLECTING ON OUR GOALS AND ACCOMPLISHMENTS

1. What was your goal for this unit (look on bulletin board or in the back of your writing notebook).

   My goal is to tell readers my opinions and ideas of a text and help them understand my reasons

2. Were you able to meet or exceed this goal? Explain. (Use examples from your own work).

   In the overall section, where it talked about my goal and the "3 meeting point," I exceeded part it to "4-exceeding."

Focus Skills

Reflective Questions

3. Look at your rubric. What is one area where you performed well in this area? What did you do as a writer to perform well in this area?

   I hooked my readers with questions facts etc. I did good as a writer by improving my information?

4. Look at your rubric. What is one area where you did not perform as well as you may have liked? What could you do *next time* to improve in this area?

   I did not perform well on test, when I got 5. I should try to use more deliberate and precise words next time.

5. Using your above reflection and your rubric, what is a goal you have for your NEXT writing piece? What will you do to meet and exceed this goal?

   I will make my words stronger, and use dictionaries to make them more precise.

6. Do you think you would like to spend 3 days improving this essay OR writing an entirely new essay? Why?

   I'd like to improve my essay. So I can try to do my goal, and improve my 3, and 3-4 mid-level by adding better function, and precise words.

Options

Deep reflection can focus on many parts of the writing process, the writing piece, and the writer. Take a day or two once every few weeks or months for this kind of reflection.

writers reread their writing searching out transitional language. The writer would highlight where he or she used it. This search in and of itself is not quite a deep reflection of writing, so Pam pairs this with reflective questions. After the search and the reflective questions, writers are given the option either to revise their piece or write a completely new one. I love this tool for its detailed lens paired with reflection and the option to take action and make choices in response to the reflection. The action is right away, not some time down the road.

One Student's Line-by-Line Reflection on His Writing

Have you ever wanted a transportation that stops at many places? Did you want it to have extra good service? Do you not only want the transportation to be luxurious but not be as expensive as 1 million dollars? Well you were lucky that you picked the perfect essay! Cruises are the most luxurious kinds of boats in the whole entire ocean. One reason why cruises are the most luxurious kinds of boots in the whole entire ocean is because they have extra good service. Another reason why cruises are the most luxurious kinds of boats in the whole entire ocean is because they dock at many places. Finally, cruises are the most luxurious kinds of boats in the whole entire ocean because they come in different sizes, shapes, and cruise lines.

Cruises are the most luxurious kinds of boats in the whole entire ocean because they have extra good service. First, cruises have room service, restaurant/buffet service and other kinds of services to make you feel good on the cruise. Second, on a cruise called MSC Splendida, I explored most parts of the ship. One place I loved was the pool deck. It had lots of things such as the towels you could just borrow with your room card. The crew members that were giving out the towels were very nice. When you're done with the towels, you just have to return it to the drop-off towel place. Also, cruises have extra good service because on Pinterest, Jessica said "Sunsets are always better on a cruise." Lastly, cruises have extra good service because the crew members don't just say the words in a serious tone and don't joke around with kids. They say it in a nice tone and sometimes a joke! On one cruise, called Star Princess, there was a in the restaurant

A color-coded reflection of writing strengths and next steps in response to the line-by-line reflection tool

---

Steps in Creating Your Own Line-by-Line Reflection Tool

1. List the important skills you taught and a symbol/color to match.

2. Add reflective questions about goals, risks, and choices.

3. End with offering the choice of revising or writing a new piece.

The many tools that are offered here as options for reflection only scratch the surface of what you can do with your students. My hope is that you find inspiration from what is here and create your own reflection experiences with students, especially when writers need learning to stick.

The power of reflection for learning is remarkable, and the options for reflection are vast. The time spent reflecting will not only give moments of pause in a busy student's day, it will also allow that glue of reflection to help learning stick. Reflection is one important instructional tool that makes learning portable—those writers who reflect are more apt to use what they have learned, about themselves and their writing, in the future and in other settings. What's more, students are happier, more invested writers, with a greater tendency to write with a growth mindset.

Techy Reflecting

Some ideas for integrating technology into your reflecting:

1. **Google Classroom** has vast resources for reflection. You may want to create a Google Form modeled after the tools shared in this chapter. Simply using the comment option on Google Docs is a techy tool. Be sure to check back to the feedback wording suggestions for tone in Chapter 3 when writing reflections for students.

(Continued)

(Continued)

2. **_Padlet_** is another interesting tech tool. One feature resembles a wall and the writer or other writers can create sticky-note-like graphics on which to jot reflections.

3. **_Glogster_** is especially robust and can be used to create interactive posters. They start you off with "edutemplates"—a virtual canvas on which writers can both publish their writing and create interactive reflections—from adding links to video or voice recordings to written reflections. Extra photos can be added, as well as a variety of other interactive features.

Conclusion

My hope is this book feels like a call to action, with tools at the ready—an eager invitation to revolutionize the sorts of feedback writers receive from the moment they place a pencil to paper until they have found their voice through owning and growing their writing identity and process, across their years of schooling. Katherine Bomer writes, "It will not help if one lone teacher in one grade level operates from a curriculum of strength and names powerful writing identities for her students and then when those students proceed to the next grade level, someone responds to their work only by circling errors in red pen" (*Hidden Gems*, 2010, p. 148). This work is too important for the well-being of our writers and now, I hope, entirely accessible and practical because of those teachers and students who have shared their successes and outcomes when the writer is the center of the writing instruction. This is a mindful approach to instruction that transforms potential frustrations into opportunities: When feeling stuck is now a reason to support risk taking, when writers hope to stretch and grow is now an opportunity for goal setting, when writers need ownership and agency is now a chance for choice making, and when it is time for learning to stick begs reflecting—this is the time to put away the red pen, both literally and figuratively, and join together so that every writer has the opportunity to write with power, passion, skill, and deep, deep awareness and gratitude for the writer within.

References

Allen, D. (2015, November 9). Growth mindset is dead. Retrieved May 28, 2016, from http://www.edutopia.org/discussion/growth-mindset-dead

Anderson, C. (2000). *How's it going? A practical guide to conferring with student writers*. Portsmouth, NH: Heinemann.

Anson, C. M. (1989). *Writing and response: Theory, practice, and research*. Retrieved from http://files.eric.ed.gov/fulltext/ED303826.pdf

Baylor, B., & Parnall, P. (1986). *I'm in charge of celebrations*. New York: Scribner's.

Black, P., & Wiliam, D. (2001). *Theory and practice in the development of formative assessment*. Paper presented at the ninth biennial conference of the European Association for Research on Learning and Instruction held at University of Freiburg, Switzerland. London, UK: King's College, London, Department of Education and Professional Studies.

Bomer, K. (2010). *Hidden gems: Naming and teaching from the brilliance in every student's writing*. Portsmouth, NH: Heinemann.

Braddock, R., Jones-Lloyd, R., & Schoer, L. (1963). Research in written composition. *NCTE*. Retrieved May 29, 2016.

Briggs, L. (1890). The correction of bad English as a requirement for admission to Harvard college. *The Academy: A Journal of Secondary Education, 5*.

Brown, B. (n.d.). Download Brené's greatly engaged feedback. Retrieved May 28, 2016, from http://brenebrown.com/wp-content/uploads/2013/09/DaringGreatly-EngagedFeedback-8x10.pdf

Brown, B. (2012). *Daring greatly: How the courage to be vulnerable transforms the way we live, love, parent, and lead*. New York: Gotham Books.

Brown, B. (2012, March). Listening to shame. Retrieved November 12, 2016, from https://www.ted.com/talks/brene_brown_listening_to_shame?language=en

Brown, B. (2015). Brené Brown: The anatomy of trust—SuperSoul.tv. Retrieved May 29, 2016, from http://www.supersoul.tv/supersoul-sessions/the-anatomy-of-trust

Calkins, L. (1980). When children want to punctuate: Basic skills belong in context. *Language Arts, 57*, 567–573. Retrieved May 29, 2016.

Calkins, L., Hartman, A., & White, Z. (2005). *One to one: The art of conferring with young writers*. Portsmouth, NH: Heinemann.

Cambourne, B., Handy, L., & Scown, P. (1988). *The whole story: Natural learning and the acquisition of literacy in the classroom*. Auckland, N.Z.: Ashton Scholastic.

Campbell, K. H. (2014, April). Beyond the five paragraph essay. *Educational Leadership, 71*(7), 60–65. Retrieved May 29, 2016.

Carter, C. (2015). *The sweet spot: How to find your groove at home and work*. New York: Ballantine Books.

Charnier-Laird, K. (2003). *Cultivating student reflection: A step-by-step guide to fostering critical thinking in young children modeled on a successful program at the Cambridgeport School by Teachers for Teachers Series, No. 6.* Dorchester, MA: Project for School Innovation.

Cole, N. L. (2015, November 9). How sociologists define human agency. Retrieved May 29, 2016, from http://sociology.about.com/od/A_Index/fl/Agency.htm

Copeland, C. T., & Rideout, H. M. (1901). *Freshman English and theme-correcting in Harvard college.* New York: Silver, Burdett and Co.

Costa, A. L., & Kallick, B. (2008). *Learning and leading with habits of mind: 16 essential characteristics for success.* Alexandria, VA: Association for Supervision and Curriculum Development.

Davies, A. (2003). *Making classroom assessment work.* Bloomington, IN: Solution Tree Press.

Denton, P. (2007). *The power of our words: Teacher language that helps children learn.* Turners Falls, MA: Northeast Foundation for Children.

DiCamillo, K. (n.d.). Kate DiCamillo's biography. Scholastic.com. Retrieved May 29, 2016, from http://www.scholastic.com/teachers/contributor/kate-dicamillo

DiCamillo, K. (2016, January 19). Kate DiCamillo. Retrieved May 29, 2016, from https://www.facebook.com/KateDiCamillo/photos/a.156440727705215.33 134.13485862734035/1244622885553655/?type=3

Diederich, P. B. (1974). *Measuring growth in English.* Urbana, IL: National Council of Teachers of English.

Di Stefano, G., Gino, F., Pisano, G. P., & Staats, B. (2014). Learning by thinking: How reflection aids performance. [John Dewey quote on reflection extracted from this paper.]

DiStefano, P., & Killion, J. (1984). Assessing writing skills through a process approach. *English Education, 16*(4), 203–207.

Duckworth, S. (2015, July 15). New #sketchnote: The Iceberg Illusion, inspired by Matthew . . . Retrieved May 28, 2016, from https://plus.google.com/ SylviaDuckworth/posts/fjVw5ZFs1Cb [modified version of Duckworth's illustration used in this text].

Dweck, C. S. (2006). *Mindset: The new psychology of success.* New York: Random House.

Dweck, C. S. (2012). *Mindset.* London: Robinson.

Dweck, C. (2015, September 22). Carol Dweck revisits the "growth mindset." Retrieved May 28, 2016, from http://www.edweek.org/ew/articles/2015/ 09/23/carol-dweck-revisits-the-growth-mindset.html

Ehrenworth, M., & Vinton, V. (2005). *The power of grammar: Unconventional approaches to the conventions of language.* Portsmouth, NH: Heinemann.

Elbow, P., & Danielewicz, J. (2008). A unilateral grading contract to improve learning and teaching. *English Department Faculty Publication Series, Paper 3.* Retrieved November 12, 2016, from http://scholarworks.umass.edu/eng_ faculty_pubs/3/?utm_source=scholarworks.umass.edu/eng_faculty_pubs/ 3&utm_medium=PDF&utm_campaign=PDFCoverPages

Elliot, A. J., & Fryer, J. W. (2008). The goal construct. In J. Shah & W. Gardner (Eds.), *Handbook of motivation science* (pp. 235–250). New York: The Guilford Press.

Facts on the teaching of grammar. Retrieved May 29, 2016, from https://www .heinemann.com/shared/onlineresources/08894/08894f5.html

Ferlazzo, L. (2014, May 2). Response: The grading system we need to have. Retrieved May 28, 2016, from http://blogs.edweek.org/teachers/classroom_qa_with_

larry_ferlazzo/2014/05/response_the_grading_system_we_need_to_have
.html?_ga=1.74731922.1876601816.144425434 [Interview with Rick Wormeli.]

Flood, J. (1991). *Handbook of research on teaching the English language arts*. New York: Macmillan. [Hillocks and Smith contributed to pp. 591–603.]

Gallagher, K. (2006). *Teaching adolescent writers*. Portland, ME: Stenhouse.

Gawron, H. W. (2011). Tips for grading and giving students feedback. Retrieved May 28, 2016, from http://www.edutopia.org/blog/grading-tips-student-feedback-heather-wolpert-gawron

Gladwell, M. (2008). *Outliers: The story of success*. New York: Little, Brown and Co.

Goldberg, G. (2015). *Mindsets and moves: Strategies that help readers take charge, grades 1-8*. Thousand Oaks, CA: Corwin.

Goldberg, G., & Serravallo, J. (2007). *Conferring with readers: Supporting each student's growth and independence*. Portsmouth, NH: Heinemann.

Gonzalez, R. (2014). The universal shapes of stories, according to Kurt Vonnegut. Retrieved May 29, 2016, from http://io9.gizmodo.com/the-universal-shapes-of-stories-according-to-kurt-vonn-1526559996

Gottman, J. (2011). John Gottman: How to build trust. Retrieved November 21, 2016, from http://www.youtube.com/watch?v=rgWnadSi91s

Graham, S., MacArthur, C. A., & Fitzgerald, J. (2013). *Best practices in writing instruction*. New York: The Guilford Press.

Graves, D. H. (1983). *Writing: Teachers and children at work*. Exeter, NH: Heinemann Educational Books.

Hansen, D. (1989). Lesson evading and lesson dissemblings: Ego strategies in the classroom. *American Journal of Education, 97*, 184–208.

Harris, R. J. (1962). An experimental inquiry into the functions and value of formal grammar in the teaching of English with special reference to the teaching of correct written English to children aged twelve to fourteen (Doctoral dissertation) [Abstract].

Hattie, J. (2009). *Visible learning: A synthesis of over 800 meta-analyses relating to achievement*. London: Routledge.

Hattie, J. (2012). *Visible learning for teachers: Maximizing impact on learning*. London: Routledge.

Hattie, J. (2013, November 22). Watch "Why are so many of our teachers and schools so successful? John Hattie at TEDxNorrkoping" video at TEDxTalks. Retrieved May 29, 2016, from http://tedxtalks.ted.com/video/Why-are-so-Many-of-our-Teachers

Hattie, J., & Timperley, H. (2007). The power of feedback. *Review of Educational Research, 77*(1), 81–112. doi:10.3102/003465430298487

Hayes, J. (1996). A new framework for understanding cognition and writing. In M. Levy & S. Randsdell (Eds.), *The science of writing: Theories, methods, individual differences, and applications* (pp. 1–27). Mahwah, NJ: Erbaum.

Heick, T. (2014, December 02). Reflecting on reflection: A habit of mind. Retrieved May 29, 2016, from http://www.edutopia.org/blog/reflecting-on-reflection-habit-of-mind-terry-heick

Henry David Thoreau. (2014, March 11). Retrieved May 29, 2016, from http://abouthenrydavidthoreau.com/269/2014/03/11/what-you-get-by-achieving-your-goals-is-not-as-important-as-what-you-become-by-achieving-your-goals-henry-david-thoreau-4

Higgins, C. (2010, November 11). J. K. Rowling's plot spreadsheet. Retrieved May 29, 2016, from http://mentalfloss.com/article/26346/jk-rowlings-plot-spreadsheet

Hillocks, G. (1986). *Research on written composition: New directions for teaching.* New York: National Conference on Research in English.

Hillocks, G., Jr., & Smith, M. W. (1991). Grammar and usage. In J. Flood, J. M. Jensen, D. Lapp, & J. R. Squire (Eds.), *Handbook of research on teaching the English language arts* (pp. 591–603). New York: Macmillan.

Hodges, T. D., & Harter, J. K. (2004). A review of the theory and research underlying the StrengthsQuest program for students. *StrengthsQuest Research: The Gallup Organization,* 190–197. Retrieved May 28, 2016, from http://www.monroecc.edu/depts/strengthsquest/documents/quest_for_strengths.pdf

John Gottman: How to build trust. (2011, October 28). Retrieved May 29, 2016, from https://www.youtube.com/watch?v=rgWnadSi91s

Johnson, B. (2014, August 07). Developing students' trust: The key to a learning partnership. Retrieved May 29, 2016, from http://www.edutopia.org/blog/student-trust-ben-johnson

Johnston, P. H. (2004). *Choice words: How our language affects children's learning.* Portland, ME: Stenhouse.

Johnston, P. H. (2012). *Opening minds: Using language to change lives.* Portland, ME: Stenhouse.

Kohn, A. (1993). Choices for children: Why and how to let students decide. Retrieved May 29, 2016, from http://www.alfiekohn.org/article/choices-children

Kohn, A. (1994). Grading: The issue is not how but why. Retrieved May 28, 2016, from http://www.alfiekohn.org/article/grading

Kohn, A. (1999). From degrading to de-grading. Retrieved May 28, 2016, from http://www.alfiekohn.org/article/degrading-de-grading

Kohn, A. (2000). Standardized testing and its victims. Retrieved May 28, 2016, from http://www.alfiekohn.org/article/standardized-testing-victims/

Kohn, A. (2010). Getting rid of grades: Case studies. Retrieved May 28, 2016, from http://www.alfiekohn.org/blogs/getting-rid-grades-case-studies

Kohn, A. (2011, November). The case against grades. Retrieved November 12, 2016, from http://www.alfiekohn.org/article/case-grades

Korbey, H. (2015, August 12). What do students lose by being perfect? Valuable failure. Retrieved May 28, 2016, from http://ww2.kqed.org/mindshift/2015/08/12/what-do-students-lose-by-being-perfect-valuable-failure

Lahey, J. (2016). *The gift of failure: How the best parents learn to let go so their children can succeed.* New York: Harper.

Lahey, J. (2015). Quoted in H. Korbey, What do students lose by being perfect? Valuable failure. Retrieved May 28, 2016, from http://ww2.kqed.org/mindshift/2015/08/12/what-do-students-lose-by-being-perfect-valuable-failure

Langer, E. J. (1981). Old age: An artifact? *Aging,* 255–281. doi:10.1016/b978-0-12-040001-0.50018-5

Learning progression definition. (2013, August 29). Retrieved May 29, 2016, from http://edglossary.org/learning-progression

Locke, E. A. (1968). Toward a theory of task motivation and incentives. *Organizational Behavior and Human Performance, 3*(2), 157–189. doi:10.1016/0030-5073(68)90004-4

Locke, E. A., & Latham, G. P. (2006). New directions in goal-setting theory. *Current Directions in Psychological Science, 15*(5), 265–268. doi:10.1111/j.1467-8721.2006.00449.x

Locke's goal-setting theory: Understanding SMART goal setting. (n.d.). Retrieved May 29, 2016, from https://www.mindtools.com/pages/article/newHTE_87.htm

Macrorie, K. (1974). To be read. *English Journal, 5*, 688–692. Retrieved May 28, 2016.

Manson, M. (2013). 3 things school taught you without you even realizing it. Retrieved May 28, 2016, from http://markmanson.net/school

Martin, A. J. (2014). Implicit theories about intelligence and growth (personal best) goals: Exploring reciprocal relationships. *British Journal of Educational Psychology, 85*(2), 207–223. doi:10.1111/bjep.12038

McMillan, C. M. (1985). Do teachers teach as they were taught to teach? *American Reading Forum, 87*. Retrieved from http://americanreadingforum.org/year book/yearbooks/85_yearbook/pdf/27_McMillan.pdf

Mezirow, J. (1990). *Fostering critical reflection in adulthood: A guide to transformative and emancipatory learning.* San Francisco: Jossey-Bass.

Miller, A. (2011). Courageous conversation: Formative assessment and grading. Retrieved May 28, 2016, from http://www.edutopia.org/blog/courageous-conversation-andrew-millertgh

Newkirk, T., & Kittle, P. (2013). *Children want to write.* Portsmouth, NH: Heinemann.

Opitz, B., Ferdinand, N. K., & Mecklinger, A. (2011, February 1). Timing matters: The impact of immediate and delayed feedback on artificial language learning. Retrieved May 28, 2016, from http://www.ncbi.nlm.nih.gov/pmc/articles/PMC3034228

Parten, M. B. (1932). Social participation among pre-school children. *The Journal of Abnormal and Social Psychology, 27*(3), 243–269.

Pearson, P. D. (2014, May). *Teaching reading: Yesterday, today, and tomorrow.* Keynote address presented at International Reading Association, New Orleans, LA.

Popham, W. J. (2008). *Transformative assessment.* Alexandria, VA: Association for Supervision and Curriculum Development.

Popham, W. J. (2011, February 22). Formative assessment-a process, not a test. Retrieved November 12, 2016, from http://www.edweek.org/ew/articles/2011/02/23/21popham.h30.html

Robinson, K. (2006, February). Do schools kill creativity? Retrieved May 28, 2016, from http://www.ted.com/talks/ken_robinson_says_schools_kill_creativity

Ronan, A. (2015, March 20). 7 ways to hack your classroom to include student choice. Retrieved May 29, 2016, from http://www.edudemic.com/7-ways-to-hack-your-classroom/

Ryan, R. M., & Deci, E. L. (2000, January). Self-determination theory and the facilitation of intrinsic motivation, social development, and well-being. *American Psychologist, 55*(1), 68–78. doi:10.1037//0003-066x.55.1.68

Shah, J. Y., & Gardner, W. L. (2008). *Handbook of motivation science.* New York: The Guilford Press.

Shaughnessy, M. P. (1977). *Errors and expectations: A guide for the teacher of basic writing.* New York: Oxford University Press.

Singer, T. W. (2014). Risk-taking is essential for professional learning. Retrieved May 28, 2016, from http://tonyasinger.com/risk-taking-essential-professional-learning/

Smith, M. W., & Wilhelm, J. D. (2007). *Getting it right: Fresh approaches to teaching grammar, usage, and correctness.* New York: Scholastic.

Stenger, M. (2014). 5 research-based tips for providing students with meaningful feedback. Retrieved May 28, 2016, from http://www.edutopia.org/blog/tips-providing-students-meaningful-feedback-marianne-stenger

Vygotskiĭ, L. S., & Cole, M. (1978). *Mind in society: The development of higher psychological processes.* Cambridge, MA: Harvard University Press.

Weaver, C. (1996). *Teaching grammar in context*. Portsmouth, NH: Boynton/Cook.

Wolpert-Gawron, H. (2011). Tips for grading and giving students feedback. Retrieved November 12, 2016, from https://www.edutopia.org/blog/grading-tips-student-feedback-heather-wolpert-gawron

Wormeli, R., & Ferlazzo, L. (2014, April). Dissecting grades: What do they mean, what are they worth? Retrieved November 12, 2016, from http://www.bamradionetwork.com/classroom-q-and-a/1927-dissecting-grades-what-do-they-mean-what-are-they-worth

Index

Notes

Notes

Notes

Notes